DEMOCRATIC DESPOTISM

DEMOCRATIC DESPOTISM

By
RAOUL E. DESVERNINE

*"Those who would give up essential
liberty to purchase a little temporary
safety deserve neither liberty nor safety."*
—BENJAMIN FRANKLIN.

DODD, MEAD AND COMPANY
NEW YORK   1936

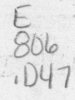

PRINTED IN THE UNITED STATES OF AMERICA
BY THE CORNWALL PRESS, INC.
CORNWALL, N. Y.

To

MY SON

GILBERT L. DESVERNINE

CONTENTS

FOREWORD

THE accusation is being persistently made by many persons in this country who are generally respected for their intellectual attainments, moral integrity, and political astuteness that the Roosevelt Administration has adopted measures, is pursuing policies, and is engaged in activities, which are intended to transform our political institutions and to remodel our social and economic order, in a manner absolutely incompatible with our traditional American ideals. It is being claimed that the New Deal has a clear and definite tendency toward the Totalitarian State, in one or other of its modern European versions: Fascism, Nazism, or Sovietism.

No more serious political accusation could be made against any individual or group, either in or out of public office, and its seriousness demands that the accusation be studiously investigated.

Having personally witnessed the early events which led to the triumph of Mussolini and of Hitler, and being more than just theoretically acquainted with their technique and objectives, this accusation aroused in me such an interest that I resolved to explore the teachings and to analyze the activities of the New Deal, to learn what, if any, basis there was for this accusation. My interest was stimulated by the fact that I was being brought professionally into contact with the actual workings of the New Deal. I offer this book as a summation of my inquiry.

As far as possible, I have chosen the method of letting some of the official leaders of the New Deal speak for themselves and explain their ideas and actions in their own words. I have called attention to the decisions of the courts comparing some of the chief items of their legislative program with the principles of our constitutional system and have briefly recorded the attitude of the courts. My personal comments and interpolations represent the opinions of one schooled in, and devoted to, the political philosophy and the ideals of freedom established by the authors of Americanism.

It is my hope that the contradictions and incompatibilities between the two schools of political thought—Americanism and the New Despotisms; Constitutional Democracy and the Totalitarian State —may become as real and vital to my readers as they are to me. If I have helped the reader, even in a small way, better to understand the real issue presented by the accusation, my purpose has been well served.

I have intended to express no opinion as to the wisdom or the feasibility of the social and economic aspects of the problems discussed, but only as to their political and constitutional implications and consequences. My concern is primarily with principles, not personalities.

This volume is a recapitulation of what is being generally said, presented in such a way as to aid us in extracting and understanding the political principles involved. The persistent refusal of the New Dealers to debate the political issues involved in their proposals, and their skilful efforts to limit all discussion to the purely social and economic aspects of their professed objectives, is simply a plea of confession and avoidance and evades the issue which is the subject of this book.

RAOUL E. DESVERNINE.

New York, N. Y.
April 7, 1936.

CHAPTER I

THE CHALLENGE

Despotism is being imposed upon great modern nations and on masses of mankind by the subtle manipulation of democratic processes and the distortion of democratic ideas, and a virtual slavery has evolved from the institutions men hoped would set them free. This menace of a disguised despotism now hangs over the political institutions of America and threatens the individual liberties of our people.

Political witches are brewing a variety of isms in the international cauldron. When brewed, men imbibe these isms, blindly trusting to their magic, not so much from the new strength in men but from their weakness. New labels have been applied to ancient and discarded panaceas. Symbols, slogans, and salutes have been borrowed from the historic past, and with uniforms of black and of brown, new messiahs have forged new autocracies on the anvil of distress and fear. Political theories and methods long since scrapped have been resurrected under new disguises, and a hodgepodge of ancient political philosophies and systems now appears under new appellations.

Sovietism, Nazism, Fascism, and Kamalism, are simply modern national adaptations of the old and all-embracing Totalitarian State in which the citizen is but a robot. They contribute no new conceptions of governmental technique. And thus it is evident that these reversions to outworn systems are reactionary, not progressive.

These ideas of the Totalitarian State are now spreading over all the world and we Americans can easily fall a prey to their allure. Circumstances make us vulnerable.

Internationally we have been brought into closer contact with Europeans and imitation has become easy. A substantial part of our inhabitants are of European birth or origin, and therefore have such similar, or receptive, modes of thinking, and such a cultural background, as to make them susceptible to foreign ideas. Our participation in the World War made us an actual party to European politics and we were vitally affected by the consequences of the political aftermath of the war. Our greatly increased interests in Europe, occasioned by our expansion in world trade and the necessity of seeking foreign markets for our surplus production, drew us into closer commercial contact with these systems. Our cultural interest in Europe, stimulated by our travel which followed the war, exposed us to the inoculation of contemporary European thought. Writings of European statesmen and publicists gained a widespread interest in the United States. America was deluged with all kinds of propaganda for every new political or economic cult. Our participation as observers in the League of Nations, and as parties in interest in international economic, labor, debt, and limitation of armament conferences, have all tended to make us world-conscious, and to tie us up with European activities.

Domestically our powers of resistance to the infiltration of these alien ideas were weakened. Every American had been sold on the idea that poverty had been conquered. He was given the assurance of economic security and the hope of a luxurious life. And then—suddenly and violently he was precipitated into one of the most serious economic depressions in the history of the United States: certainly within his life and memory. This led him to believe that the economic and political system under which he had been living was either antiquated or had failed. He blamed our economic ills on our political institutions. He started to reappraise his values; to doubt the principles which he heretofore had accepted as obvious, even axiomatic. Naturally, he, in his disappointment and desperation, was prone to embrace any panaceas offered. In times of stress and strain, it is a human weakness to seize upon old disguised solutions for seemingly novel problems.

The American stage was set for a challenge to the existing order by those ambitious to bring about a change in our political institutions. Economic restoration was being promised through political transformation. All our economic and social ills were to be met by political means. We were surrounded by a sea of "new" philosophies. The American mind was being almost imperceptibly prepared to receive these new ideas. They seemed to be just part of the world in which we are living. Disease often spreads into an uncontrollable plague because its germ is not soon enough recognized, isolated, and arrested; and because man's power of resistance has been weakened.

Abroad empires and kingdoms had been violently transformed into republics, communistic states, and dictatorships. Some kingdoms were made empty and meaningless symbols for dominating groups. In some nations, there was a rapid rotation of monarchies and republics. Under some parliamentary systems, cabinets changed with the rapidity of men passing through a revolving door.

Only England and France, among the great historic nations of Europe, have successfully resisted political breakdown in the midst of fundamental economic disasters. England was saved by her traditional-ism; France has until now survived through her intense nationalism.

English tradition is personified by her king and

emperor. Not only does he unite in one common national destiny all subjects of a widely scattered commonwealth, of different races, creeds and interests; but also he represents to each British subject the symbolized custodian of all the individual liberties won by Englishmen, from kings and feudal lords, from the time of the Magna Charta to the present day. This succession of principles of individual rights and national ideals—this deposit of the political faith of their fathers—is what is popularly called English tradition. Every Britisher is so jealous of this tradition that he instinctively defends it; its violation simply "isn't cricket." Even though the British Parliament is, in legal effect, omnipotent, it is, for all practical purposes, limited to the exercise of only those prerogatives which are not inconsistent with tradition. At least, no British Government has yet dared to risk giving a challenge to the fundamentals of English tradition.

France, to a lesser degree, has evolved, not so much a traditional-ism, as a nationalism. It has built up a Culture, in which every Frenchman takes a great national pride. Frenchmen boast of and cherish the "Rights of Man," proclaimed and won in the French Revolution. These ideals are deeply imbedded in French character, and French character is individualistic, realistic, and nationalistic; and is rarely carried away by emotional outbursts. Her nationalism is

intensified by the conservative instincts of her pre-
dominating agrarian population and the general fear
of change under the threat of another war. Although
French parliaments may occasionally, and ministries
constantly do, change, national ideals and principles
are unaffected. "Liberty, fraternity, and equality,"
the slogan of his individual rights as a Frenchman,
have thus far not been impaired.

In America, our tradition is constitutionalism.
The Constitution is our emperor, our king. It is our
political Culture.

English tradition was the preceaent, and French
social philosophy the inspiration, of our Constitution.
English traditional-ism, French nationalism, and
American constitutionalism are all founded upon,
and have as their authoritative sanction, the confidence and allegiance of the people. So far, this popular confidence and allegiance has not been destroyed,
and, for that reason, these nations still retain their
political institutions intact.

The challenge of the New Despotism in every
instance has been against the established order,
against the traditional authority, whatever the form
that authority had taken in any particular country.
The people demanded something, anything, different,
any escape from the status quo. The direct challenge
has always been preceded by organized, but usually
concealed and indirect, maneuvers to break down

public trust and confidence in existing national institutions.

Our tradition has always been identified in the public mind with constitutional concepts. We have developed no political tradition or culture entirely independent of our constitutional thinking. Any attack on these concepts is, therefore, far more serious here than in other countries. Change in political forms is one thing, but change in political philosophy is quite another. We can safely alter our political machinery, if we do not thereby destroy the substance of our political system and ideals.

Tradition is our anchorage to the past, our ballast in the present, and it should be our compass for the future. In distress an experienced mariner might jettison his cargo to save his ship, but he certainly would not throw his chart, compass, and rudder overboard; and leave himself adrift without any knowledge of, or control over, his direction.

The challenge at present being made in America is against the very foundations of our political institutions and against the organic structure of our constitutional system. The issue is clear cut. It is the issue of:

Constitutional Democracy—Americanism

vs.

The Totalitarian State—The New Despotism

Can those two diametrically opposed systems be made to live together? Can they possibly be harmonized? Or must not one ultimately destroy the other, and reign supreme? That is the implication contained in the statements, now being heard daily, that American-ism is incompatible with Fascism, Nazism, Sovietism, and Kamalism, or with any other form of the totali-tarian state.

By all this world confusion, coupled with all our domestic anxiety, we have been thrown into an intel-lectual whirl in our political thinking. Our only safe course is to recall first principles as a guide to our future judgment, or, at least, not to abandon them without serious reflection. We must be rational, not emotional. Society has not progressed to that ideal state where it can live an orderly and beneficial exist-ence without the restraint and discipline of some authority, and without rationalization by some defin-ite criteria. Mere motion is not necessarily progress. We must choose a definite destination. We must fasten ourselves to fixed ideals.

We are being told that the issue is simply one of party affiliations, organization allegiance. This is pure nonsense and can only be intended to confuse our thinking and thereby to divert us from the real issue. It is significant that traditional Republicans and tra-ditional Democrats now find themselves aligned together. On the other hand, many of the discontented and of the innovators not only of these two parties but outside of them have now found a common meeting ground. Except for those who seek patronage or personal benefit from organization regularity, the line between two basically different schools of political thought is being sharply drawn. The issue is one of principle, not of parties; the contestants are divided, irrespective of parties, on the bases of their political philosophy and of their attitude toward the Constitution.

Furthermore, we are not witnessing merely a revival of the old controversy between the advocates of a centralized system and of a decentralized system. Even the most rabid Federalists never advocated an unlimited and absolute Federal Government. It was then only a question as to how much power the Federal Government must be given to make a union of autonomous States a practical and workable union. But, as a matter of fact, the Jeffersonians have now become Hamiltonians and the Hamiltonians, Jeffersonians. The party of Jefferson has now even outdone Hamilton in that the Roosevelt Administration has attempted to absorb the States into the Federal Government and thereby make the Federal Government omnipotent. Hamilton never advocated the complete obliteration of the sovereignty of the States, which the Supreme Court has stated that the Roosevelt Administration has legislatively attempted. Who could ever have imagined that the Republican Party would be the defender of the States' Rights against the Democratic Party? This paradox well illustrates the confusion in our current political thinking.

Ideally, a political party organization has one function and one only. It is the democratic instrumentality by which the party ideal is advanced. If the party forsakes its principles then it becomes not a political party in the true American sense, but purely an instrument for the self-aggrandizement of its partisans.

The two-party system has been our greatest political stabilizer. Throughout our history each party has had a distinctive creed, so that a choice between opposing theories and ideas has always been presented to the people. The pros and the cons of great political issues were thus always debated for public enlightenment and selection. This is no longer true. The Democratic and Republican parties no longer have any distinctive ideals and characteristic platforms. All shades and kinds of political thought are to be found in each party. Fundamentally, a Republican Hoover and a Republican La Follette, a Democratic Carter Glass and a Democratic Huey Long, cannot possibly be put in the same respective political categories. On the other hand, a Republican Hoover and a Democratic Glass are in substantial accord; so, similarly, are a Republican La Follette and a Democratic Huey Long. Their present alignment is purely a partisan accident, not a political conviction. The two parties have become purely "His Majesty's Government" and "His Majesty's Opposition." It is a fight between the ins and the outs: a struggle for control.

We do not intend to suggest that this has no utility. It, indeed, exposes the program of the controlling faction to the criticism of the opposition; which is publicly enlightening, but with the persistence of party labels, and with the sharpened contrasts between the actions of partisans and the ideals of their parties, confusion mounts. We must not make a fetish of mere party names. Our political parties have ceased to have their old significance. They are now merely a means to power.

Moreover, we experiment with a variety of proposals advanced to meet economic and social emergencies and to promote reform and recovery; we passionately debate specific legislative enactments; driven by expediency we are fighting over the "today," without any thought of the "tomorrow"; and, above all, we are so blinded by the *details* of our immediate interests that we are making decisions, selecting courses, and adopting methods without any consideration of the underlying principles involved. We are losing sight of the possible permanent political consequences of our economic and social experimentation. Let us be sure we clearly understand the implications of our present activities! Let us be sure we understand the consequences of some of the departures from our settled political philosophy! Finally, let us always evaluate each proposal, each law, each activity, not only on its own merit, but in its relationship to all others, and measure all individually and collectively by the standards of our institutions and of their effect, if any, upon them.

It does not necessarily follow that economic reconstruction requires political reconstruction. England has been able to meet the challenge of economic distress within the framework of her traditional institutions and without destroying historic liberties.

We must not be deceived! The challenge today is not to party loyalties and platforms; the issue is not between one piece of legislation and another, this proposal or that. The challenge is to the very foundations of our two traditional political institutions— Inalienable Individual Rights, and Self-Government —and to their organic and structural framework; a Federal union of autonomous States. This challenge is so fundamental that our whole future depends upon how we meet it.

Let us now define Americanism, and then proceed carefully to consider the vital principles and basic institutions which are its very Soul.

CHAPTER II

WHAT is this thing called "Americanism"? Is it just an adaptation of foreign political ideals to the soil of America? Is it just a revised copy of some parent civilization? Or, is it basically a new and characteristically distinctive theory and system of government? Has it a character, a personality, all its own? What do we Americans mean when we so proudly boast of being Americans? That we live within the territorial confines of a certain area of the earth's surface called America? Or, that we have a political faith and a national individuality of our own conception and creation, which we now cherish and will defend as a tradition, and look to for salvation?

Many forms of democracies have risen and fallen. Many forms of democracies presently exist. Experiments in democracy have long been carried on in all times and under all conditions, and a comprehensive and expensive experience has been gained by patient and long-suffering mankind in its struggle to find a political system most expressive of its ideals and most promising for its needs.

Our Founding Fathers were not experimenting at random when they created our particular kind of democratic government. They made a rational selection based upon historical precedent and upon their own actual experience. They had certain basic concepts, which they not only strove to express, but, more important, also to guarantee to all Americans, so that these would forever be the proud possessors of certain rights and liberties not then elsewhere enjoyed.

Ours is not a pure democracy in which the people rule themselves, either directly or through unrestrained representatives, and in which the will of the majority alone governs. That system the Founding Fathers wisely rejected. Ours is a Constitutional Democracy in which the majority is restricted by definite constitutional limitations, and in which the States and the individuals are guaranteed certain rights, expressly reserved to them and placed beyond the power of the majority. The English system of an omnipotent parliament, practically disciplined by tradition, but, nevertheless, theoretically unrestrained by a written covenant with the people, did not meet the requirements of the Founding Fathers. In the prerevolutionary seethings in France they foresaw the perils of an uncontrolled majority. Their consuming ambition was to make the Freedom of Man indestructible. They therefore sought and found an immutable anchorage, an eternal sanction,

for man's individual liberties. Obviously, this had
to be beyond man's reach, and there is no other such
anchorage but God.

Our political philosophy was, therefore, conceived
and founded upon the basic principle that man as a
creature of God has been endowed by his Creator
with certain physical and spiritual characteristics,
attributes, and natures, and that to these certain
rights appertain, in fact are inherent in, and are an
integrant part of, man's very nature itself. Let us
illustrate. As man has been endowed by his Creator
with reason and free will, he is possessed of a natural
right to personal liberty, which is simply the exercise
of free will. As man has been endowed with the duty
and instinct to worship, he must be free to perform
this duty and exercise this instinct according to the
dictates of his own conscience, which is the natural
right of freedom of religious worship. As man has
the thirst for knowledge and the capacity to impart
instruction to others, he must have the natural right
to education. As man has been endowed with the
capacity, and the duty, to propagate his species, and
as his children are physically incapable of self-sustenance during infancy, then certainly nature has or-
dained that he may fulfill this obligation by the most
suitable means, the family. As nature obliges man to
sustain himself, and to provide for those naturally
dependent upon him, he must have the natural right

to produce, acquire, and possess those physical things
—property—necessary for the fulfillment of these
obligations.

There are other human rights, which are not so
clearly an intrinsic part of man's physical nature, but
which are equally essential to his spiritual nature, and
without which he would cease to be Man, as we
understand Man.   Human experience has demonstrated that certain rights are indispensable to an
individual if he be not a political slave.   These rights
have been won by man through the centuries in his
struggle for freedom against his political masters.

As Man is older than the State, some of these natural rights of his likewise are pre-existent to the State,
and therefore cannot be said to have originated with
the State, or to be grants or franchises from the State.
This being so, they are by their nature above and
beyond the State.   That is why they are called inalienable.   Even Man himself cannot surrender or transfer
them without doing violence to his nature.

To deprive Man of these other rights which he has
acquired in his struggle for freedom, is to reverse the
order of history and to destroy the primal concepts
of the civilization which man has built through the
ages.   We should hesitate before we undertake to fly
in the face of all human experience.

Now, these philosophical principles are part of our
organic law.   The Declaration of Independence itself

proclaims it as a self-evident truth that man was endowed by his Creator with certain inalienable rights. This is certainly an unequivocable declaration as to the divine origin and affirmation of these basic rights. We too often think of the Declaration of Independence as only an indictment against a tyrannical government, specifying certain violations and abuses of individual freedom, and fail to get its real significance as a proclamation of the natural and historic rights of man, essential to his liberty and his birthright as an American. It is a declaration of the minimum essential rights of man in a free self-governing state.

The importance of the Declaration of Independence to one trying to understand the fundamentals of our political tradition cannot be overestimated. Although the Supreme Court of the United States has said that the Declaration of Independence cannot be considered as having "the force of organic law, or to be made the basis of judicial decision as to the limit of right and duty, and while in all cases reference must be made to the organic law of the nation for such limits," nevertheless, the organic law—the Constitution—"is but the body and the letter," of which the Declaration of Independence "is the thought and the spirit, and it is always safe to read the letter of the Constitution in the spirit of the Declaration of Independence."

Thomas Jefferson, the author of the Declaration of Independence, received most of his inspiration for the form and substance of that noble document, and obtained much of the teaching he so forcibly set forth therein from the new school of French political philosophers, who were then intellectually inflaming France for the coming revolution. These ideals were vividly before his eyes and had become a vital part of him. It was indelibly impressed upon his mind that their acceptance was the only means of protecting individual freedom from the tyranny and oppression of governments and majorities. He had been taught to distrust all governments. Individual liberty had become an obsession with him.

We may easily imagine his amazement, therefore, when upon his return from France, he saw for the first time the proposed Constitution of the United States, and found no recital therein expressly reserving the inalienable rights of man to the people and expressly putting these beyond the power of the Federal Government unduly to interfere with. In spite of the fact that the reservation of these basic rights was considered to be implicitly contained in the original Constitution, and in spite of the fact that they were established in most of the State Constitutions, he insisted that these basic rights must not be entrusted to implication or interpretation, but must be safeguarded by express constitutional reservation.

It was greatly at his relentless urging that the first ten amendments to the Constitution, popularly called the "Bill of Rights," were adopted, and it was not until their adoption had been assured, in the case of several States in the act of ratification itself, that the Constitution finally became effective. Jefferson molded the entire philosophy of the Declaration of Independence into the Constitution, and thereby justly earned the title, the "Apostle of Americanism."

It is strikingly significant that Thomas Jefferson although so dominated by French political philosophy, departed therefrom by one fundamental innovation. The French and American revolutions were both in principle a struggle against excess and abuse of royal prerogatives. They were both begun by proclamations of the rights and liberty of men, but in the French proclamation such rights were *not* asserted to be endowed by God. They were supposed to be based upon compact between man and man. Rousseau called this "The Social Contract." The individual, however, gave up his will when he made a Social Contract and the State became omnipotent, containing in itself absolutely all the rights of all the citizens who composed it. In America, the people refused to make any such contract. They refused to give the State an absolute power of attorney. They cautiously reserved the rights they deemed essential to their individual freedom, and, furthermore, they did not accept the principle that these rights originated from contract among men.

Now, these basic human and individual rights are not impracticable metaphysical abstractions and imaginary ideals found in philosophical treatises, as many would have us believe. They are real and are substantially defined and expressly enumerated in the Constitution, particularly in the First Ten Amendments. They have been read into and have been made a part of our organic law. They are the vital principles of our constitutional system.

Briefly, they are: Religious liberty; freedom of speech and of the press; right of the people peaceably to assemble and to petition the Government for a redress of grievances; the right to bear arms; the citizens' right of privacy and security, in their persons, houses, papers, and effects, against unreasonable search and seizure; the right of trial by jury and freedom from excessive fines and cruel punishments; and finally that no one shall be "deprived of life, liberty, or property, without due process of law."

The irreducible minimum of civil rights essential to political freedom, in the judgment of the Founding Fathers, are those collected in the Bill of Rights. They collectively compose Man's political integrity.

But freedom requires even more than the possession of these civil rights; it demands independence. Freedom is a reality, or it is nothing. Man is either independent of the State or he is a mere dependent of the State.

An illuminating example of how demagogic word-twisters try to deceive the people into surrendering their rights is found in their beguiling declaration: "Human rights are above property rights." Now, the fact is that property rights are human rights. A property right is the human right to acquire, possess, and use property. Property is one of the realities of freedom and is so classified by the Founding Fathers. Ownership of property has been historically identified with freedom. Property ownership was the distinction between the freeman and the serf. Man not only gained his political freedom but also his economic freedom by the use of property. Although this conception originally applied to real property only, it is now understood to embrace the more diversified types of property which have become of equal or greater utility as a result of the changed economic conditions.

As a matter of fact the word "property" as used in the Constitution has been judicially defined to mean the "exclusive right to possess, enjoy, and dispose of . . . everything subject to ownership, . . . real or personal," "everything which has an exchangable value," including the right to labor, to transact business, to contract, and "all rights and powers incident to ownership." All economic enterprise is now just as much property as is land. It equally produces the means to self-sustenance, to independence. Deprive man of the fruits of property and he becomes dependent. If the State alone possesses all property, or completely controls its use, then man becomes a ward of the State. Control over use of property may be so far-reaching as to render title to property a mere fiction: an empty right. Legal ownership may not always be effective ownership. Therefore, the measure of control which the State exercises over the use of property is the determining factor as to whether or not alleged control is not in effect confiscation. This truism becomes of great import in our later considerations.

It is because of this historic, political, and economic relationship between property and freedom that the Founding Fathers expressly included property in their enumeration of essential individual rights. The Supreme Court once characterized property as "the arch upon which civilized government rests," and said that "this once abandoned, everything was at stake and in danger."

No sensible person denies that each citizen has social responsibilities and community obligations which impose certain restraints upon his exercise of his personal rights, but the method by which the Government may impose such restraints *must* be consistent with the Constitution.

It is inconceivable how the Founding Fathers could have more dogmatically and unequivocably proclaimed and established the principle that there are certain individual rights above the power and jurisdiction of government, and that this was not only a fundamental principle of, but even in the nature of a condition precedent to, the very creation of our constitutional system.

This principle has received the official authentication of the Supreme Court in the following striking language:

"It must be conceded that there are such rights in every free government beyond the control of the State. A government which recognized no such rights, which held the lives, the liberty and the property of its citizens subject at all times to the absolute disposition and unlimited control of even the most democratic depository of power, is after all but a despotism. . . . The theory of our governments, *state and national,* is opposed to the deposit of unlimited power anywhere. . . . There are limitations on such power which grow out of the essential nature of all free governments."

Another "self-evident" truth of Americanism, proclaimed by the Declaration of Independence, is: "all men are created equal." This does not mean that all men are equal in their natural perfections, but only that they are equal in their right to liberty. We must not confuse political equality with natural equality.

This means that all the *people* of the United States, regardless of race, color, or creed; irrespective of social class, financial means, or propertied interests —the factory worker, the farmer, the industrialist, the financier, the professional man—all who are part and parcel of the social, economic, and political unity of the nation have an equal political right to, and constitutional guarantee of, the benefits of the institutions of our government. All have equality of civil rights under the Constitution and before all the laws of the land. Even the criminal is entitled to his day in court and to due process of law. The sacred principle of democratic government is denied by anyone who uses the power of public office to stir up class conflict, to oppose class against class, to make it appear that the economic or social interests of one group are opposed to those of others, and that all cannot live and work together toward a common national destiny. Thus to stir up domestic internal strife is no less vicious than it is to rattle the saber in international relations.

The Declaration of Independence also enunciates the doctrine that "governments derive their just powers from the consent of the governed." This proclaims the institution of self-government. This doctrine establishes two basic principles: first, that the people are the ultimate repository, and the source, of sovereign power; and second, that, therefore, government must derive its power from the people, and, consequently, can have only such powers as are expressly granted it by the people. Hence, the State is the creature of Man, not Man the creature of the State; and the State cannot exceed its granted powers without thereby committing an act of tyranny, for tyranny is only the usurping of powers against the consent of the governed.

This is an underlying principle of all our governments, both Federal and State. It is the cornerstone of our political freedom. Once concede that government has powers not expressly granted it by the people, or which are not indispensably necessary to carry those powers into effect, and you have removed the first American bulwark against despotism. Implicit in the theory that a State has certain inherent sovereign prerogatives just because it is a State, is the first step in the transfer of sovereignty from the people to the State.

The Constitution itself emanates from the people. It is not the declaration of the thirteen individual States made, jointly and severally, in their sovereign capacity, but emphatically as its preamble declares it is the act of the sovereign people. Its very first words are: "We the People of the United States . . . do ordain and establish this Constitution for the United

States of America." This is a clear recognition and acknowledgment by express recital of the doctrine that ultimate sovereignty resides in the people and in the people alone, and that the Constitution must have the sanction of, and a mandate, from the people, to have any just validity. In fact, in American political philosophy, there can be absolutely no such thing as State sovereignty unless it be based on the underlying sovereignty of the people. Chief Justice Marshall, speaking for the Supreme Court in *McCullough vs. Maryland,* said: "The government of the union, then . . . is emphatically and truly a government of the people. In form and substance it emanates from them, its powers are granted by them and for their benefit." The Constitution is simply the means through which the sovereign people constituted and defined the government to which they consented. It is a power of attorney constituting the government their agent for certain specified purposes: granting certain express powers and proscribing others. By it a nation was born: the United States of America became a reality as a nation. Until the Constitution was adopted, the nation was such only in name. The Articles of Confederation by which the Colonies were bound together were "but a rope of sand" and only created a league of independent sovereignties, not a nation.

The Declaration of Independence significantly says

that governments are instituted to the end, and for
the purpose, of securing these institutions of inalienable rights and of self-government, and that consequently the people have the right to alter or abolish
the form of their government when it "becomes
destructive of these ends." Clearly, under such doctrine, the State is not an end in itself, but is a mere
means to an end; and, therefore, if it seeks other ends
than those assigned, if it appropriates unto itself
some unappointed mission and employs implements
in the achievement of this not expressly given to it,
no matter what the apparent motive may be, we
must pause and carefully consider whether or not
these new "ends" are destructive of the original
"ends" of our institutions. In a word, are we being
diverted from our American objectives by men, who,
pretending to have a new vision, are setting up new
objectives to which we have not yet given our sanction or our mandate? The people in the exercise of
their sovereign prerogatives have the supreme right
to determine the "ends" of their government, to select
the ideals and character of their institutions. They
have given clear expression to those "ends," to those
ideals. Also, they have prescribed the only way in
which these may be changed.

Directly to challenge or even indirectly to attempt
to impair these principles—of Individual Rights and
of Self-Government—is to attack the very foundations

of American tradition and the vital principles of our constitutional system. *These two institutions of Individual Rights and of Self-Government are the Soul of Americanism.*

Now let us look at the organic structure, the Body of Americanism!

CHAPTER III

PROPERLY to understand the true nature and real significance of the form and structure of our government, we must view it as the physical organism and governmental mechanism, which give to the living principles of our political philosophy the mechanical body and the instrumentality that enable such principles to live, move, and have their being.

Our Founding Fathers were so obsessed with the necessity of safeguarding individual freedom from every possibility of governmental oppression, that they deliberately designed a scheme of government under which governmental prerogatives were so decentralized and scattered that no single political unit had sufficient power vested in it to give it the potentiality of oppression. They not only tried to put man's liberties beyond the reach of government, but they also tried to make government impotent legally to assail them. They were confident that without such a plan of government, the mere pronouncements of these rights would be futile. Their attitude toward the kind of Federal government they desired can best be analytically illustrated by observing the notable fact that there are only twenty grants of power to the Federal government in the Constitution, whereas there are thirty-one prohibitions against, and restrictions on, the exercise of power.

They fully understood, of course, the need of constructing an efficient and workable system. They had many historic patterns before them from which to select, and many experiences to enlighten them. They molded, and added to, old democratic forms to fit the necessities of their own political ideals.

Now let us briefly look at the framework and the structure of our government in the light of these ideals, so that we may appraise all proposed modifications, and, perhaps, expose the concealed motives behind much of the tinkering and tampering that is now going on.

The Constitution clearly establishes, and differentiates between, the two separate and distinct jurisdictions: of the Federal Government and of the State governments. We cannot exaggerate the importance of this segregation of jurisdictions. The debates in the Constitutional Convention, the Federalist Papers and all other similar contemporary writings, and, above all, the reluctance with which some States ratified the Constitution, feature this as a fundamental characteristic. Court decisions, political platforms and campaigns, even civil war, have revolved around this issue. It is deeply imbedded in our history. Even those who advocated a strong centralized Federal Government never sought the complete denial of State sovereignty.

The question was only one of degree; that is to say, the extent to which it was deemed necessary or advisable to implement the Federal Government with power adequate to promote the common and united interests of the States without destroying the autonomy of the States, or so to encroach upon or to curtail their powers, as to make them incapable of local self-government.

The boundary lines between Federal and State rights were more pronounced then than now. The thirteen original States were individually more or less self-contained and each was to a large extent economically self-sufficient. Trade between them was more a convenience than a necessity. Each had its own colonial history and had, therefore, developed a distinct political individuality and a somewhat different set of traditions. Each had a pride in its own independence. They had a diversity of social and economic problems, occasioned by differences in climate, in the national origin and racial characteristics of its inhabitants, and in other conditions, which made local self-government necessary to meet different local requirements. And above all, they had bitterly suffered from political "absentee landlordism" and they well knew the necessity of having the sovereign and the citizen live in close proximity. Distant sovereigns did not understand local needs and they became irresponsible because they could not readily be made accountable.

Now, geographical boundaries often seem arbitrary and do not necessarily constitute cultural, social, or economic units, but our tradition of a Federal union of autonomous States was predicated on sound reasons.

Undoubtedly the expansion of the country, the development of instrumentalities of intercommunication, the sectional diversity of production, and the interdependence of different sections, on the products and the markets of others, all tended to lessen this separateness and to integrate the States economically, socially, and politically. Our foreign trade and our international interests have increased our need for greater unified national action. All of this is admitted, and obviously the mere form of government must yield to the substance of its objectives, but when the concentration of power in the Federal Government transcends mere matters of form, and tends to obliterate the States and to break down our Federal system, then this is a matter of substance, not of form. We cannot deny that our Courts have clearly recognized the necessity for greater integrated action, and have greatly expanded the Federal powers by giving to certain provisions of the Constitution a liberal interpretation to meet the exigencies of new conditions, *but* always within definite confines, and always cautiously preserving the sovereignty of the States and scrupulously respecting the constitutional divisions of power.

Those who maintain that our Federal system is antiquated and is no longer adequate under changed conditions, must take upon themselves the burden of proving their contention, and thus far the convincing proof has not been produced. That the formula they have selected to accomplish their objectives is prohibited is not proof that the objectives could not be attained through permissive formulas. In addition, they have not yet proven that the objective itself is desirable. Furthermore, many advocates of the necessity for change simply do not understand our system, or deliberately refuse to comprehend its essential characteristics.

Unfortunately, even President Roosevelt evidently labored under such misconceptions in his criticisms of the *Schechter* decision, when he expressed the feeling that our government was far behind the governments of Europe in dealing with problems of social welfare. This criticism overlooks entirely the true nature of our government. It confuses the Federal Government with what *our* government really is—a composite of Federal, State, and local governments—all of which must be taken together in order to understand what actually constitutes *our* government. It assumes that what the Federal Government cannot do, must remain undone. This is the view of one so dominated by the concepts of the modern European State that he has failed to learn, or has forgotten, the real nature of the American Federal system.

A restriction against Federal action in no way demonstrates that our government is impotent to take action. It merely shows that the Federal Government is not the proper division of the government to act in that case—unless, of course, it is also shown that the State or local governments are equally unable to take the action. There is no reason to assume that, because some powers are given to State and to local governments rather than to the central or Federal Government, our government as a whole is less effective or less powerful than the more centralized governments of Europe. To show surprise that all governmental powers are not vested in the Federal Government completely overlooks the true nature of our government, and fails to recognize not only the powers but also the duties of the several States to provide for local matters. The United States Supreme Court in the *Schechter* decision clearly recognized that the government of our people consists of more than just the Federal Government, and that the respective duties of the State and of the local government should be duly respected. At no place did the Court indicate that it proposed any limitation on governmental action as such; but it did indicate a dividing line between the powers and duties of the two divisions of our governmental system.

When considering the powers of *our* government, the sovereign powers of the several States are of as much importance as the centralized powers of the Federal Government. Each has its proper sphere of action, and to look only at one is to overlook the carefully planned system of our government as a whole. We fear that those who have been guilty of this misconception are making their wish the father to their thought!

The Supreme Court itself perceived that this erroneous conception of our governmental system existed in the minds of the draftsmen of some of our recent legislation and it took the occasion in the recent *A.A.A.* case to refresh their recollections. It said:

"The question is not what power the Federal Government ought to have but what powers in fact have been given by the people. It hardly seems necessary to reiterate that ours is a dual form of government; that in every state there are two governments,—the state and the United States. Each State has all governmental powers save such as the people, by their Constitution, have conferred upon the United States, denied to the States, or reserved to themselves. The federal union is a government of delegated powers. It has only such as are expressly conferred upon it and such as are reasonably to be implied from those granted. In this respect we differ radically from nations where all legislative power, is vested in a parliament or other legislative body subject to no restrictions except the discretion of its members."

The Supreme Court even seems here to find it expedient to make the comparison between our system and foreign systems, as if it were aware that confusion existed in the minds of some as to their distinctive differences.

The powers of the Federal Government have been wisely restricted to those expressly granted to it, and to those necessary and proper to carry such granted powers into effect. Moreover, wanting to remove every vestige of doubt as to the limitations of the Federal Government, even at the expense of supererogation, some of the States, before they would ratify the Constitution, insisted on publicly declaring that they were consenting to its ratification only because of their confident belief that it would be promptly amended so as to provide, among other things, that "powers not delegated to the United States by the Constitution, nor prohibited by it to the States, are reserved to the States respectively, or to the people." This is an omnibus rider attached by an over-cautious lawyer, and clearly shows what he was trying to guard against!

Another proof of the distrust the Founding Fathers had for the concentration of power in a highly centralized government, is their further effort to dilute even the limited power granted the Federal Government by splitting its exercise up into separate, independent, and equalizing units, by the creation of three distinct co-equal departments—the legislative, the executive, and the judicial branches—each having definitely enumerated functions and each being a check upon the other. Here again, this segregation and allocation of power was not designed purely as a matter of mechanical convenience of procedure, but as a further check and restraining influence on the possibility of abusive or excessive exercise of delegated power. It was also an attempt to guard against coercive practices, or, the dominating influence, of a too-strong executive, or of an over-zealous or "politics-ridden" legislature.

Although many times assailed, and recently with powerful onslaughts, the sanctity of the separateness of these three governmental branches has always been, thus far, effectively defended and safeguarded.

The meticulous care with which the authors of the Constitution strove to keep all possible political implements of oppression under the direct control of the people is peculiarly illustrated by the fact that of all legislative functions conferred on Congress the most important one from the point of view of their experience—the right of taxation—was broken up between both houses of Congress, so that all tax measures must originate in the House of Representatives, and be approved by the Senate as well as by the House. The colonists had learned only too well the oppressive effects of "taxation without representation." They knew that the power to tax is the power to destroy. Therefore, this power must reside directly under the people's control. The members of the Senate were originally regarded as the spokesmen of Sovereign States; more or less as Ambassadors from foreign potentates. They were chosen by the State legislatures for a six-year term. The members of the House of Representatives were, on the other hand, the direct representatives of the people and were elected every two years by popular suffrage. They were, therefore, immediately and directly accountable to the people and had to go to the people every two years for re-election on their respective records.

Certainly our Founding Fathers were distrustful folk—distrustful of government—and jealous of their freedom. What prophetic foresight they had! If they could return today and witness taxation transformed into coercive penalties, submission to the sovereign will purchased by tax rebates, and taxation elaborated into confiscation, they might wonder if they had not labored in vain.

Our Founding Fathers also well knew that although in some aspects of government the majority will should have full expression, nevertheless, freedom demanded certain curbs on the mere power of numbers, to assure individual liberty from the possible tyranny of majorities as well as from the caprices of the sovereign. They tried to balance popular will and individual liberty.

The House of Representatives was to express the majority popular will. Its members were to be elected directly by the people on the basis of numerical representation. This was the only branch of the government to be the direct voice of the people. The Senate was to represent the equal sovereignty of the States, irrespective of the population of any State, thereby safeguarding States' rights, and the unit equality of each State, against both centralized tyranny and the weakness of the representative system. Senators were appointed by the State legislature. Even the President and Vice-President were not to be directly elected by the people: the people only selecting electors to the Electoral College which elected the President and Vice-President. This interposed between the popular will and the election of the President and the Vice-President the independent judgment of the electors, thereby assuring that such election was to be by a group of substantial citizens free from the enthusiasms and passion of the mob. The Judiciary was, of course, completely removed from popular selection and was made a matter of Executive selection with Senatorial approval. The House of Representatives was significantly deprived of any voice whatsover in the designation of judges. The authors of the Constitution well knew that to preserve a government of impersonal law, those applying the law had to be completely divorced from political agitation and pressures, and had also to be politically unaffected by the consequences of their judgments.

The original system of Presidential election by independent electors has been subverted. Now such electors are firmly committed to vote for a particular candidate, so that we have, for all practical purposes, elections of the President and Vice-President by direct popular vote. The Electoral College has thus become an empty form. Senators, by constitutional amendment, are now also chosen by direct popular vote. Therefore, with both Houses of Congress and the Executive Branch of the Government so chosen, every branch of the Government, except the Judiciary, now is chosen by majority-will. This already represents great progress toward pure democracy and is a considerable departure from the constitutional democracy, designed by the Founders of our nation. Obviously, the next attack must be made on the Judiciary if pure democracy is to supersede constitutional democracy. This attack is frequently made and takes many forms: popular recall of judicial decisions; popular election of judges for limited terms; and depriving the courts of the power of invalidating legislative and executive action.

We observe this in passing only as an evidence of an apparent increase in popular desire for a pure democracy—the rule of mere numbers—and to accentuate the fact that our Founding Fathers did not have a great trust in such a political system, and were in fact apprehensive of a "tyranny of a majority." Fully to understand the underlying philosophy of our system, we must not be unmindful of the great caution with which our ancestors approached any political formula which contained the possibility of trespassing on their individual independence.

The recent ascendency of the executive power over the legislative is to be noted with alarm. Strong personalities who naturally dominate come into power. Emergencies and special circumstances, such as war, often justify an expansion of executive power. We may be complacent during the existence of emergencies but we must be vigilant lest emergency sacrifices be converted into permanent surrender of our substantive rights. And then let us not be forgetful of the fact that thus far our Constitution has proved adequate in peace and in war. Let us be sure that the emergency cannot be met by means *within* the Constitution before we even temporarily condone any departure from it!

Washington in his Farewell Address eloquently sounded the warning against the concentration of power as a prelude to despotism. Here are his words of warning:

"It is important, likewise, that the habits of thinking a free Country should inspire caution in those entrusted with its administration, to confine themselves within their respective constitutional spheres; avoiding in the exercise of the powers of one department to encroach upon another. The spirit of encroachment tends to consolidate the powers of all the departments in one, and thus to create whatever the form of government a real despotism. A just estimate of that love of power, and proneness to abuse it, which predominates in the human heart, is sufficient to satisfy us of the truth of this position. The necessity of reciprocal checks in the exercise of political power; by dividing and distributing it into different depositories, and constituting each the Guardian of the Public Weal against invasions by the others, has been evinced by experiments ancient and modern;—some of them in our country and under our own eyes. To preserve them must be as necessary as to institute them. If in the opinion of the People, the distribution or modification of the Constitutional powers be in any particular wrong, let it be corrected by an amendment in the way the Constitution designates. But let there be no change by usurpation; for though this, in one instance, may be the instrument of good, it is the customary weapon by which free governments are destroyed. The precedent must always greatly overbalance in permanent evil any partial or transient benefit which the use itself can at any time yield."

And so we see that the architects of our government designed our whole Constitutional edifice to be built on a foundation calculated to protect the freedom of all trusting to its shelter from the storms of governmental oppression and the assaults of arbitrary majorities. Let us be certain, therefore, that those who attempt or propose any remodeling of the United States Constitution, under the claim that our life will thus be made more secure and abundant, are not seeking entrance to undermine the very foundations of our governmental edifice! At least, let us examine and judge all such efforts in the light of a true understanding of the real intendment of our constitutional structure.

The Constitutional form and structure of our government is but the habitation and life mechanism of the sacred principles of Americanism—it is the Body of Americanism.

Now, let us turn to the Conscience of Americanism, that which rationalizes, disciplines, and judges the validity of its activities—the Judiciary.

CHAPTER IV

AMERICANISM—ITS CONSCIENCE

THE Constitution is the solemn covenant of the Federal Government with the people, guaranteeing the people their liberties, and setting up a machinery for self-government. The Constitution, therefore, is the means through which the sovereign people constituted and defined the government to which they consented. It is the popular expression of the rationalization of our political philosophy. It is the supreme expression of the sovereign will. Because of its supremacy our government is correctly characterized as a government of laws, not of men.

It is self-evident that the government has no political or moral right to repudiate, to violate, or to evade this solemn compact with its citizens, or to alter or amend it without the citizens' voluntary and express consent. Should the Federal Government attempt to appropriate powers reserved to the States or to the people; should any branch of the Federal Government attempt to exercise powers not assigned to it, at the expense of trespassing upon the jurisdiction of the States, or of another department; and should any branch of the government attempt to delegate to another powers specifically entrusted to it; in each of such cases the result is not a mere technical and unsubstantial departure from constitutional procedure, but is a wilful violation of a solemn obligation and contract.

Now, this conception of the contractual basis for governmental authority and powers had existed and gradually grown up for one hundred and fifty years before the ratification of the Constitution, and as a political principle had become deeply embedded in the American mind.

The rights and liberties of the colonists as British subjects were guaranteed by royal charters, the grantees of which were prohibited by the express terms of the charters from passing laws or issuing orders which were repugnant to those of England or which exceeded the granted powers. These charters conditioned their grants of land on the acceptance of, and the obedience to, the charter terms. These charters only remotely determined the forms which the colonial governments should assume, or what the rights of the colonists should be, but they implanted the idea in the minds of the colonists that they must look to their Charter for the origin and scope of their powers. Furthermore, the colonists, as British subjects, were mindful of the historic English practice of reducing to written covenant, or declaration, all rights won by Englishmen from their sovereigns and lords. Obviously our colonists were bound to be charter-conscious: constitution-conscious. They were accustomed to look to their written contract to determine their rights when political controversy arose between them and their government. This is the origin of our theory of constitutional government.

Later, when the colonies separated from Great Britain, the first thing they did was to establish State Constitutions safeguarding, against State Legislative despotism, those human rights which they regarded as fundamental, and defining a scheme of local self-government.

We must, therefore, observe that constitutionalism was a historic tradition and a life experience for the authors of the Constitution. Founded in English history, and developed in America through the Colonial Charters and State Constitutions, this conception prevailed. Is it difficult to realize, therefore, the sanctity this idea had in the minds and hearts of the Founding Fathers?

Now, since the relationships between the government and its citizens, and of the citizens with one another, are contractual, it is perfectly obvious that there must be some power somewhere to interpret the contract when dispute arises and to enforce it when violated. Without such power, the contract would at best be a moral obligation respected only by the virtuous or used at will by the strong against the weak. Can a holiness justifiably be attributed to governments which individuals have been unable to attain? To do so we must be infinitely more trustful of government than our political ancestors were, and we must be blissfully ignorant of the lessons of history. This power of interpretation of the contract between the people and the government of this country—the Constitution—is confided to the United States Supreme Court.

For this reason, the only means by which the system established by the Constitution can be maintained, and our individual freedom be made secure from government infringement, lies in the doctrine that the courts have the right to challenge the validity of legislative and executive acts and to declare them unconstitutional, that is to say, in violation of the terms and conditions of the political contract. If the judiciary be deprived of this power the Constitution becomes a mere "scrap of paper"; and there will then have been removed the last guarantee of our liberties. Our whole tradition will be endangered!

It makes none but an academic and technical difference whether the Supreme Court was expressly given this power, or whether this power was developed by logical deduction from expressed powers, or, as some argue, whether this power was usurped by the court by its own declaration. The simple fact is that unless somebody has the power to adjudicate all controversies arising under the Constitution, then there is absolutely no means of assuring that the Constitution will be respected by anyone.

But so that the record may be kept straight, let us point out that the State Courts had asserted and exercised the power of interpreting and of enforcing the respective State Constitutions without there being any specific provisions in those Constitutions expressly authorizing such action, and that the framers of the Federal Constitution were aware of all this. The State Courts claimed this power as an absolutely indispensable prerogative by implication and as being essentially inherent in the conception of a Constitution. Therefore, there was no particular reason why the framers of the Federal Constitution should deem it necessary expressly to provide this provision in their Constitution. It was a recognized and accepted practice.

This is all merely of historical and academic interest, but it has no practical importance whatsoever. This power has been exercised and has been popularly acquiesced in, even if not welcome, since it was first pronounced by John Marshall in the case of *Marbury vs. Madison*. Unless the citizen has recourse to the courts for the protection of his rights, and unless the courts have plenary power to grant him adequate relief, the mere assertion of his rights is a sham. No one who respects the Constitution, and wants to live under it, would have any reason for not welcoming the determination by the courts of all controversies arising out of it. If the people choose not to allow the Supreme Court this power, they can at any time so determine through the prescribed constitutional method of amendment.

This is an unique characteristic of our governmental system, significantly distinguishing it from all others, and it conclusively demonstrates the extent to which our system goes to keep the government within the strict confines of constitutional limitations. Judicial review of legislation and executive action may well prove our most important contribution to the science of government.

Briefly, the Supreme Court of the United States is the guardian of those vital rights of civil liberty, which it is its duty under the Constitution to protect against infringment by Federal or State legislatures or executives, and it preserves the organic structure and framework of the government against destruction at the hands of an assuming legislature or executive. It keeps the Federal Government and the State governments within their respective constitutional confines and the three branches of the Federal Government within the limits of their assigned functions. Deprive it of these functions and our entire constitutional system, and the rights it confers, exist only at the sufferance of the majority, and the Soul and the Body of Americanism have no assured permanency.

Certain current misconceptions of our judicial system must be corrected or we shall be led to regrettable conclusions by erroneous reasoning.

Mr. Justice Stone, in his dissenting opinion in the *Hoosac Mills Case*, involving the constitutionality of the Agricultural Adjustment Act, urged caution and self-restraint upon judges, and warned them not to be hasty in setting aside acts of Congress. He said that the Courts must not consider themselves superior to other branches of the government in the "capacity to govern." The Courts do and should rightly consider themselves superior in the capacity to decide whether disputed laws exceed the constitutional power of Congress, or whether challenged executive action exceeds the constitutional functions of the Executive. To confuse, as Mr. Justice Stone in the *Hoosac Mills Case* did, *judicial* action with *governing* action under our system is to display an absolute lack of appreciation of the true nature of our judiciary. Our judiciary does not *govern* in any sense of that word, it simply rationalizes and validates our conduct with constitutional concepts. It performs an act of comparative analysis in comparing a legislative enactment, or an executive action, with the Constitution and determines if they gibe. It is the searching Conscience of Americanism.

The true function of the Supreme Court has recently and clearly been restated by the Court itself in its decision in the *Hoosac Mills Case* as follows:

"When an act of Congress is appropriately challenged in the courts as not conforming to the constitutional mandate the judicial branch of the Government has only one duty,—to lay the article of the Constitution which is invoked beside the statute which is challenged and to decide whether the latter squares with the former."

The courts have no general power to veto, or to set aside, acts for unconstitutionality. In fact, by far the greater number of violations of the Constitution never reach the Supreme Court. The judicial power is only the power to decide justiciable controversies (law-suits) and to render judgments binding on the parties to such controversies. Being thus limited to deciding the rights of the parties to particular cases, it would be unthinkable that courts would have to adjudge those rights according to an invalid act of the legislative branch, and not according to the "Supreme law of the land." The power of the courts to adjudicate rights according to the Constitution is implicit in the declaration that the Constitution is the supreme law and no one in the Constitutional Convention doubted that it was so intended to be, and was. If the courts claimed a *general* power to review and set aside acts of a co-ordinate branch, they would have to point to a specific grant of such power, but the grant of judicial power was ample to authorize its exercise according to the law of the land.

No decision has ever been rendered or ever can be rendered, by the Supreme Court, right or wrong, which can block any public objective desired by the people. The Supreme Court only determines whether or not Congress or other officials have acted within the Constitution. The people always have the right to take whatever action they wish with respect to the amending of the Constitution, and the decision of the Supreme Court that Congress or other officials have exceeded constitutional limitations is in effect nothing but a decision that the matter should be turned back to the people and passed upon by them through a Constitutional amendment. In other words, instead of denying the right of the people it refers the matter back to the people. The people have several times exercised this right by amending the Constitution to authorize action which had been previously judicially disallowed.

This power in the Courts has taken on an increased importance in view of the number of laws

recently enacted by Congress in excess of its constitutional power, and of the Executive's urging the
passing of laws of doubtful constitutionality.

The proposals in Congress, and the threats by
zealots aligned with the Administration, to deny to
citizens recourse to the courts, or to deny to the
Supreme Court the right of review, display a pal-
pable ignorance of our judicial system and would
be futile to accomplish the purposes intended. They
are none the less mischievous and if adopted would
result in endless confusion.

Article VI, Section 2, of the Constitution is a man-
datory requirement that the Constitution shall be
the supreme law of the land, binding not only upon
the Congress, the Executive, and the Federal Judiciary, but providing also that the "Judges in every
State shall be bound thereby." If power to declare
invalid laws or acts is denied by Congress to the
Federal Courts, or the power of the Federal Courts
to interpret and apply the Constitution be impaired,
citizens would still have recourse to their State Courts
to redress violations of the Constitution attempted
either by Congress or by the Federal Executive.
Those who are seeking and advocating freedom from
judicial restraint by the simple device of legislatively
imposing restrictions on the functions of the Federal
Courts, and thus impairing their efficacy to require
compliance with the Constitution, totally ignore this

provision of the Constitution, and labor under the delusion that they can accomplish their objectives by simply legislatively restricting the jurisdiction of the Federal Courts.

The real question is whether the Constitution shall by final recourse to the Supreme Court be capable of final and uniform interpretation, right or wrong, but known and understood, or whether the Constitution shall be left to the uncertainty of the decisions of the tribunals of forty-eight different States, and to scrambling conflicts between the States and the Federal Government.

It should be evident that without a single tribunal for the final interpretation of the Constitution, there would be, in effect no Constitution; that the rightness or wrongness of a decision is of less practical importance than its certainty; and that there is a rational and orderly remedy for erroneous interpretation; but that there is no such remedy for the disorder and civil strife, which would accompany the curtailment of final review by the Supreme Court.

Furthermore, the Supreme Court, because of the finality and nationwide application of its decisions, gives definiteness and uniformity to, and equalizes, the status and rights of all American citizens. Without it we would have no single standard for American citizenship, but would have instead forty-eight different standards of State citizenship.

The Constitution cannot be maintained as the *supreme* law of the land unless its supremacy can be protected. Contemptuously to characterize the Constitution as a super-government is to advocate the substitution of a government of men for a government of laws. It is an effort to destroy qualitative freedom and erect quantitative freedom in its place. It would deprive citizens of the guarantee of their liberties and would leave them at the mercy of the arbitrary will of a majority.

The effort now is to frame legislation so that no question can arise that the courts can pass on. If successful, there would be no means available to assure individual rights in accordance with the law of the land. We would have a mere constitutional proclamation of such rights but no way of ever enforcing their recognition or enjoyment. A right without a remedy is a sham, a pretense. This attack against the judicial power goes to the very heart of Americanism and imperils our institutions and freedom more than any other single challenge could. Its possible consequences to our personal liberties cannot be over-emphasized.

The Supreme Court has well expressed the need for judicial restraint upon governmental power as follows:

"The limitations imposed by our constitutional law upon the action of the governments, both state and national, are essential to the preservation of public and private rights, notwithstanding the representative character of our political institutions. The enforcement of these limitations *by judicial process* is the device of self-governing communities to protect the rights of individuals and minorities . . . against the power of numbers."

The clear cut question is presented whether we shall be ruled by law or by arbitrary will. It is the age-long struggle between protected liberty and despotism. The choice is ours, but let us thoroughly understand the consequences of the choice we make.

We have, therefore, seen that the Constitution is a living organism, with soul, body, and conscience; it is the living force in our political lives, shaping our political destiny; it is our political personality: in short, it makes us Americans. Remove it and we would become shapeless and wandering political ghosts. We would become mere material capable of taking on any form under the molding of men having the power to cast us in the die of their designs, so as to utilize us for their purposes. But every living organism has certain basic characteristics and physical attributes and these cannot be altered without destroying the vitality of the organism or substituting a distinctively different organism in its place. These inherent and characteristic attributes we have explained. Let us carefully weigh the proposals of those who would have us believe that our Constitution is a fossilized and antiquated exemplar of the political philosophy of a glorious past age: a document which should now be relegated to our historical archives! The Constitution recognizes Man as God's creature resplendent with the victories and progress of civilization. The New Despotisms, as we shall observe, propose to re-create man according to the superior pattern of man's new vision.

We should, therefore, now take a glance at the New Despotisms!

CHAPTER V

THE NEW DESPOTISMS

FASCISM, Nazism, Sovietism, and Kamalism are, as has been said, simply modern adaptations of the old Totalitarian State molded and remodeled to fit the political needs and thinking of certain dominant political groups now ruling respectively, Italy, Germany, Russia, and Turkey. Although their actors, costuming, language, and scenery, may greatly differ, they, nevertheless, are all playing the same old drama —"Despotism." The people seem so enthralled with the play that they are still unconscious of the fact that their freedom is its price. Each of these dramas has a prologue of promise and an epilogue of despair. They all have the same theme and the same moral. Let us briefly review the story of these "puppets who put shackles on the liberties of the people."

Fascism, Nazism, and Sovietism began in the activity of small groups of men wholly convinced that they alone knew the solutions for their respective national political and economic problems; and that they alone were competent to restore government to the people; the nation to its international destiny; and economic, social, and political liberty to man. Their ideals are all the same.

They all rode into power on solemn promises to the people of great social and economic benefits to come to them, and, less openly, on promises to their supporters of jobs and patronage.

In their party platforms, they promised the solution of the agricultural problem; to cut the costs of government; to reduce bureaucracy and taxes; to provide social security; and to restore political liberty.

They were all confronted with a gullible people, so their task was comparatively easy. The World War left economic distress, social and political disintegration, international disappointments, and popular despair scattered over the face of all Europe. National ideals were confused and national traditions challenged. How human to blame all this on the old governments and how natural to embrace any new government which brings new promises and new hopes!

As soon as they became confident that they were solidly entrenched in power, they "discovered" that their platforms had already become antiquated by the rapid progress made under their impetus, so these platforms were relegated to their national historical archives and new chapters "in the history of popular government" were written. It is these new chapters which we must study, and so become vigilant to detect and recognize similar tendencies whenever and wherever they confront us.

In Italy, Germany, and Russia the record shows that government costs and taxes greatly increased; bureaucracy spread like a flame; the agricultural problem remains unsolved; social security has been translated into social dependency and political liberty into political slavery. But the promises made by these leaders of jobs for their supporters have been most generously fulfilled. They purchased allegiance with promises, doles, and jobs. They rewarded the faithful, and they organized these into an army of political shock troops, and from this selected their "Corporal's guards." They slowly built up an exclusive self-perpetuating governing class. They well knew that their popularity must wane and that they could continue in office only by force, not by persuasion. An intolerance to opposition ripened into the destruction of opposition. Forcibly to stamp out all opposition becomes the main measure of self-defense and self-preservation always adopted by despots.

The Fascist party in Italy numbers around 2,500,-000 members out of an entire population amounting to 42,000,000. In Russia the Communist party numbers less than 2,000,000 out of a total population of about 170,000,000. In the Nazi party there are about 2,000,000 members in a population of 62,000,000. These minorities are highly privileged and are absolutely dominating. They have no opposition. They have the "one-party system" and these minorities are the party workers. A citizen either belongs to that party, or is disenfranchised and becomes a political outcast.

Those who would like to imagine just what a similar "one-party system" would be like in America, should hastily look at these comparable figures. In the United States at the last election it was estimated that the combined total of the active members of the Democratic and the Republican parties was around 1,500,000 in a population of 129,000,000. It is easy to imagine what the consequences would be if these 1,500,000 active party members were the only ones who could effectively vote, or otherwise be politically active, instead of the 38,000,000 men and women who actually did vote in 1932.

And so we see the remarkable similarity in the origin, methods, progress, and results of these isms. It is important to observe that they were all started with popular approval, acquiescence, or submission and gradually develop into political systems in which the people are not consulted, but subjected. They are governments without, and in some instances against, the consent of the governed. It is for this reason that we have classified these isms as the New Despotisms. They are the political antitheses of democracies.

The fundamental political philosophy of these New Despotisms is even more important and more indicative of their nature than are their political tactics and strategy, because therein is revealed the character of the State they seek to perfect and perpetuate, and, more especially, the ideal of human freedom they are striving to attain.

Let us now briefly recall the pronouncements, platforms, and principles proclaimed by the acknowledged masters of these New Despotisms; cull therefrom their ideals and ideas; and thus learn the direction in which they are traveling.

A. FASCISM

The march on Rome was practically unanimously acclaimed and supported. The whole nation responded to the call to rectify the injustice done Italy in the failure of the Allies adequately to reward Italy, as promised, for her war sacrifices, and to salvage the country from political chaos. Fascism certainly received a popular affirmation. It was an emotional and dramatic expression of the will of the people. Mussolini captured the imagination of the Italian population by his courage, his boldness. He personified the nation's ambitions and ideals.

Mussolini, nevertheless, on his triumphal arrival in Rome immediately pledged his allegiance to the

Kingdom and its King. He sought to legitimatize his action with the stamp of royal sanction. He did not think of himself as an usurper of governmental prerogatives, but rather as a leader selected by the manifestation of popular will and with the constitutional and traditional sanction of the established dynasty.

It seems certain that Mussolini's intentions were good; they were patriotic. In his first official program, published in 1919, he promised the decentralization of the executive power, the rule of the people, the nationalization of the credit system, the "suppression of every kind of speculation," the closing of the Stock Exchange, the payment of the national debt by the wealthy, and even the abolition of military conscription. That was in 1919. Three years later Mussolini was in power, and his previously proclaimed ideas had completely changed. By 1923 he was so intoxicated with power that he even dared to say: "It (fascism) has once passed and if needful will turn to pass again over the more or less decomposed body of the Goddess of Liberty." By 1928, he had control of 100 per cent of the Chamber. The Chamber was now no more than his audience, his claque. His Ministry, the Grand Council of the Party, the National Fascist Federation, the National Council of Corporations, are only names, are all just his creatures, are Mussolini.

The men of opposition parties have been exiled,

imprisoned, in many instances killed. The press is completely controlled. Literature, universities, and schools, are regimented, as all history, law, economics, and philosophy, must be instilled into the public mind in the spirit of Fascism. The children are taught a new history, a new faith—"I believe in the genius of Mussolini, in our Holy Father Fascism," is the quasi-ecclesiastical language in which he expresses his idea that the State is supreme, not only politically, but also spiritually.

In his magazine, "Hierarchy," (March, 1923), Mussolini is brief and to the point in rejecting all the "liberal" ideas of the nineteenth century and in sneeringly scrapping liberty itself: "Facts are worth more than books; experience more than doctrines": constitutes his dogmatic declaration of this theory. Developing this thought he says: "Now the greatest experience which has come to us after the World War . . . is the defeat of liberalism. In Russia and in Italy it has been shown that it is possible to govern outside, above and against the whole of liberalism's idealogy. Both Communism and Fascism are outside the bounds of liberalism. . . . Liberty is not an end; it is a means. As a means it ought to be controlled and dominated. . . ."

"Now Fascism," he continues, "throws all these anti-vital theories to the scrap-heap. When a group or a party is in power it is obliged to fortify itself and to defend itself against all comers. The truth, plain to the eyes of all who are not blinded by dogmatism, is that men are tired, perhaps, of liberty. They have had an orgy of it. Today liberty is no longer the severe and chaste virgin for which generations of the first part of the last century fought and died. For the intrepid youth who, uneasy and alert, face the dawn of new history there are other words which have greater fascination; these are, order, hierarchy, discipline. The poor Italian liberalism, which goes in search of a greater liberty, groaning and struggling is very much behind. It is quite outside all understanding and possibility. . . . Let it be known then, once and for all," Mussolini concludes, "that Fascism knows no idol, worships no faith; it has once passed, and if needful, will turn to pass again over the more or less decomposed body of the Goddess of Liberty."

Article Eight of the Fascist decalogue—a designation which reveals that Mussolini, like so many other Italians, still has the smell of the sacristy about him, provides: "Mussolini is always right," and Article Ten: "One thing you must hold dear to you above all—the life of the Duce."

The credo of the youth organization—The Balilla —a document denounced as sacrilegious by the Bishop of Brescia with the approval of the Vatican, is a beautiful example of the tendency of the neo-tyrants of our "modern" dictatorships to take on a supernatural quality: This Credo is thus expressed:

"Q. What does it mean to be a Fascist?
 A. It means that the commandments, precepts, and sacraments of Italy must be observed.
 Q. What is its creed?
 A. It is the creed given by the Apostles of Italy and of Fascism.
 Q. Of how many articles does it consist?
 A. Of twelve articles, as follows:
    1. I believe in Rome Eternal, mother of my fatherland;
    2. And in Italy, her first born;
    3. Who was born of her virgin womb by the grace of God;
    4. Who suffered under the barbarian invader, was crucified, slain and buried;
    5. Who descended into the sepulcher, and rose again from the dead in the nineteenth century;
    6. Who ascended to Heaven in her glory in 1918 and in 1922 (by the March on Rome);
    7. Who is seated at the right hand of Mother Rome;
    8. Who will come thence to judge the living and the dead.
    9. I believe in the genius of Mussolini;

10. In our Holy Father Fascism and in the
    communion of martyrs;
11. In the conversion of the Italians; and
12. In the resurrection of the Empire.
    Amen!"

"Fascism is a spiritual way," says Mussolini in his
article, "Fascism: Its Theory and Philosophy," in the
Treccani Italian Encyclopedia. And farther along
in this article: "For the Fascist everything is within
the State, and nothing human or spiritual exists, and
much less has worth, outside of the State. It is in this
sense that Fascism is Totalitarian, and the Fascist
State, synthesized and united by every value and
worth, interprets, develops and strengthens the whole
life of the people. . . . The Fascist State, the most
potent and highest form of the personality is a force,
but a spiritual one, which sums up all the forms of
man's moral and intellectual life. It cannot therefore be limited to simple governmental functions of
order and protection, as liberalism used to desire.
Fascism is not a simple mechanism which limits the
sphere of supposed individual liberty. It is an interior form and norm and a discipline of the whole
person; it permeates the will like the intelligence.
Its principle, a central inspiration of the human personality living in the civic community, descends
deeply and lodges in the heart of the man of action as

well as the thinker, of the artist as well as the scientist; it is the soul of the soul."

As if in a blare of trumpets, he concludes, "Fascism then is not only a giver of laws and a founder of institutions, but an educator and promoter of spiritual life. It demands to remake not the forms of human life, but the contents; man, character, faith. And to this end it demands a discipline and authority which descends within the spirit and there dominates unchallenged. . . ."

And still Fascism marches on! It is now even weeping for more worlds to conquer.

B. NAZISM

Nazism arose out of the bitterness of the aftermath of the World War, the degradation of defeat, and economic and political despair. An empire of which all Germans were proud: too proud; which had fought itself to national greatness and international importance, yes, almost supremacy, crashed by its own weight and ambition, and left its subjects humiliated by defeat; their national ideal crushed; and its people scrambling to find some new ideal, some new order, to give them comfort, stability, and hope. The German Constitution had not supplanted the Empire in the hearts and minds of the people. It was not a vitalizing force, but was simply the forum of political experimentation carried on by changing governments with shifting policies.

Hitler, like Mussolini, rose to power emotionally. He directed his appeal to the people's desire for security, for restoration, both national and international. His courage challenged the attention of a cowered people. He did not dramatically capture the government by a theatrical march on Berlin, but slowly won popular support through the democratic process of electioneering and elections. He could have taken power sooner had he willed so to do, but he insisted upon, and finally received, the approval of the people at the polls. His government, therefore, has a constitutional sanction and a popular mandate.

Once in power his platform under the Constitution became a philosophy dictated by his will. His respect for democratic methods shown in his rise to power was before long, when in power, distorted into dictatorship. The Nazi dictatorship ran true to type: regimentation of education and of the press, the destruction of all opposition, the denial of individual liberty itself, the absorption of the citizens by the State, and the persecution of disfavored races, characterize its policies. Dictatorships are ever thus!

As Bismarck found his model in Cavour, so did Hitler find his in Mussolini. There are differences—personal, and otherwise—notably Hitler's emphasis on race, but politically one must have a mind for legalistic subtleties to note any substantial dissimilarity. Hitler shares with Mussolini, Stalin, and Kamal a profound hatred for human liberty. His fundamental political ideal is theirs: "one party, one pattern, one rhythm, one creed," as Dr. Gooch so epigrammatically expressed it.

The most characteristic bit of spoken "totalitarianism" from the lips of Hitler is his comment, June 30, 1934, after the execution without trial of scores of his political opponents. As he put it with descriptive eloquence: "For twenty-four hours I have been the Supreme Court of the German Nation." In a phrase, the dictator embodies in himself all judicial procedure, traditional, constitutional, and statutory: is free from all judicial restraint and is the final judge of his own conduct.

The Dictator is also the source of all substantive law, as well as of all procedure, and is infallible in their pronouncement and administration, and prescribes all parliamentary formula for the enactment of the one and the establishment of the other. General Goering thus enunciates this doctrine in his book, "Germany Reborn": "We Nazis believe that in political affairs Adolf Hitler is infallible. . . . His will is my law."

In Hitler's autobiography, "Mein Kampf," the Bible of Nazism, we read the following:

"The youth movement is in its essence and organization anti-parliamentarian; i.e., it rejects, in principle and in its composition any theory of the majority vote implying that the leader (the dictator) is degraded to being merely there to carry out the orders and opinions of others. In small things and great, the movement stands for the principle of unquestioned authority of the leader, combined with fullest responsibility. . . . For the task of organization is to communicate a definite idea—which always originates in the brain of one single man—to the general public, and also to see to its conversion from theory into reality."

Hitler's "Mein Kampf" can best, in his own words, depict his fundamental political ideals and processes; so let us read a few excerpts. We shall begin with the passage that classifies the inhabitants of the state in the following terms:

"The national State divides its inhabitants into three classes: State citizens, State subjects, and foreigners. In principle birth only gives the status of a subject. This does not carry with it the right to serve yet as a State official nor to take active part in politics in the sense of voting at elections. In the case of every State subject race and nationality have to be proved. The subject is free at any time to cease being a subject and become a citizen in the country corresponding with his nationality. The foreigner is only different from the subject in that he is a subject in a foreign state."

Both interesting and instructive is the description that "Mein Kampf" gives of the education which the Dictator has decreed must be imposed on every young native German subject:

"The young subject of German nationality is bound to undergo the school education which is laid down for every German. Later on he must consent to undergo the bodily exercises as laid down by the State, and finally he enters the Army. Military training is universal. After his military service is over, the healthy young man with a blameless record will be solemnly invested with the rights of State citizenship. This is the most important document for his whole life on earth. It must be held in greater honor to be a citizen of this Reich, even if only a crossing-sweeper, than to be a king in a foreign state."

The "control of majorities," the "Fuehrer" thus summarily, and conveniently, disposes of:

"The national State must work untiringly to set all government, especially the highest—that is, the political leadership—free from the principle of control by majorities, that is, the multitude—so as to secure the undisputed authority of the individual in its stead." The best form of State and constitution is that which with natural sureness of hand raises the best brains of the community to a position of leadership and predominant influence. There must be no majority making decisions, but merely a body of responsible persons, and the word 'council' will revert to its ancient meaning. Every man shall have councillors at his side, but the decision shall be made by the one Man."

Hitler provides the National State—himself—with expert advice in these words, tinged perceptibly with Mussolini's "Corporative idea":

"The National State does not suffer that men whose education and occupation have not given them special knowledge shall be invited to advise on or judge of subjects of a specialized nature, such as economics. The State will therefore subdivide its representative body into political committees and committees representing professions and trades. In order to obtain advantageous cooperation between the two, there will be over them a particular Senate."

In the following few lines Hitler confides to the world his ideal of a model Legislative Branch of government:

"But neither Senate nor chamber will have power to make decisions; they are appointed to work and not to make decisions. Individual members may advise, but never decide. That is the exclusive prerogative of the responsible President for the time being."

Probably with the wish to relieve himself of the

disagreeable necessity of constituting himself for another twenty-four hours the Supreme Court of the German nation—Blood purges are, at best, a messy business—Hitler issues a warning to his enemies in the following frank fashion:

"A world theory (such as Nazism) is intolerant and is not content with being one party among a number of other parties; it insists on exclusive and persistent recognition of itself and on an absolutely new conception of the whole of public life in accordance with its views. Thus it cannot tolerate continuance of a force representing the former conditions. ". . . Political parties are always ready to compromise; world-theories never are. Political parties bargain with their opponents; world theories proclaim that they themselves are infallible."

The Fuehrer certainly pipes no uncertain sound when he declares:

"Our standpoint has always to be that of high national policy, and must never be narrow or particularist. This last observation is necessary lest our adherents should come to imagine that we National Socialists would think of denying that the Reich has a right to assume a higher sovereignty than that of the individual states. There neither should nor could be any question as to that right. Since for us the State in itself is but a form, whereas the essential is that which it includes—namely, the nation, the people—it is clear that everything else must be subordinated to the nation's interests; and in particular we cannot permit any single State within the nation and the Reich (which represents the nation) to enjoy independent political sovereignty as a State. The doctrines of National Socialism are not meant to serve the political interests of single States of the Confederation, but to lead the German nation. They must determine the life of a whole nation and shape it afresh; they must therefore peremptorily claim the right to overstep boundaries, drawn according to political developments which we have rejected."

Nazism, therefore, has in its brief political life written and proclaimed the gospel we have set forth and explained in the past few pages, and has, by the sword, subjected all Germany to its obedience. The Empire was succeeded by the Republic, and the Republic, by—Hitler!

C. SOVIETISM

We now view another of the New Despotisms—Sovietism. It fundamentally differs from Fascism and from Nazism in that it did not rise to power by popular acclaim or by popular votes, and therefore cannot claim a popular sanction or mandate. It seized power by violence, by revolution. The fearlessness of the leaders of a small strongly organized minority of communistic zealots set them up as a government when for all practical purposes no government existed. They had a political prophet, political disciples, and a political organization in a world of political chaos. They had an economic creed as well as political ambitions. This minority gained, and holds, control over the majority solely by the strength of their unity and the weakness of the disunity of the majority.

With their economic teachings and practices we have no concern in this book. Their political principles and ideals are here our single interest.

These principles may be summed up in one brief extraordinary sentence. We quote from Hurwitz, "Fundamental Principles of the Soviet Constitution," an official book published in Moscow:

"Everything not formally allowed by the Government is forbidden."

Try as we would, we could not contrive any statement more contradictory to the American conception of Government and of individual liberty, than that made by these nine words. Here, indeed, is revealed the soul of Totalitarianism! So that we may clearly understand its implications, let us paraphrase this declaration by inserting the real meaning of its words.

Everything (*all individual rights and personal liberties*) not formally allowed by the Government (*by the arbitrary will and absolute pleasure of one man*

—Stalin) is forbidden (*not by any Constitution, law, or legal process, but by force and the terror of extreme punishment or exile*).

Hurwitz again says: "The power of the State is above all a symbol of coercion"; and he also declares: "the source and creator of all laws is the State."

Article I of the Soviet Civil Code very frankly provides: "Dictatorship is a power which relies on force: it is limited by no law, and is subject to no rules to direct it."

It is important correctly to understand the Communist's conception of the State. Engels wrote a letter to Bebel in March, 1875, and Lenin, in a manuscript, written in 1916 or 1917, quoted this letter with the comment, that he thought it the "most excellent" passage in the works of Marx and Engels "against the State." Engels in that letter wrote:

"Since the State is only a transitional institution which must be utilized in the struggle, in the revolution, in order to crush our enemies by force, it is pure nonsense to speak of a free people's State: as long as the proletariat needs the State, it needs it, not in the interests of freedom, but in order to crush its enemies, and when it becomes possible to speak of freedom, the State, as such, will cease to exist."

Although the dictatorship is here declared to be "transitional," that is temporary, but the *term* of its

duration is not stated. It will last, evidently, as long
as is necessary. This was, in substance, the answer
Stalin gave Lady Astor when she asked him how long
he would continue to kill people. As long, therefore,
as the dictator in his absolute discretion deems it
necessary, for who else is to determine! One must be
very credulous to believe that once a despot is vested
with absolute power, he will voluntarily surrender it.
History teaches that dictatorships customarily end
only with the death of the dictator or his forcible
ejection.

Stalin says in his book "Leninism": "Lenin repeatedly explained that our State is the State of the proletarian dictatorship, and the proletarian dictatorship
in the power of one class, the power of the proletariat."

Theoretically the dictatorship of the proletariat
may be the State, as Stalin in this passage of his book
reports it to be, but actually the Communist party,
with its two million members, out of a population of
140,000,000, is the State. The Government is, mys-
tically, distinct from the State. The structure of the
present Russian Government is the system of Soviets
but the Soviets are composed of delegates from only
the Communist party. In a speech in January, 1933,
at a Party conference, Stalin frankly confessed this;
his words were:

"When it is a question of responsibility and the

degree of blame, the responsibility falls wholly and entirely upon the Communists, and we are to blame for everything—we Communists alone. . . . There is not and never was in all the world such a strong authoritative power as the Soviet power. There is not and never has been such a powerful and authoritative party as our party."

Even more clearly, in his "Leninism," Stalin announces: "In the Soviet Union, in the land where the dictatorship of the proletariat is in force, no important political or organizational problem is ever decided by our Soviets and other mass organizations without directives from the Party."

And again, in the same book, he declares: "The working class without a revolutionary party is an army without a general staff. Our Party is the war staff of the proletarian army." And yet again (still quoting his "Leninism") he states: "The dictatorship of the proletariat is the issuing of directives by the Party, plus the carrying of these directives into effect on the part of the mass organizations of the proletariat, plus their being made actual by the population at large." And—now to conclude our quotations from "Leninism" on this point—he says:

". . . The Party constitutes a unity of wills which is incompatible with any setting up of factions and any division of Power." The "Party" is, of course,— Stalin.

Only those Russians are permitted to vote who are "formally allowed," provided they are not members of the "enemy classes," not peasants who resisted collectivization, not the clergy, not religious workers, not employers of others for profit; provided, in short, they are not anybody who dares to act, even to think, in opposition to the dictatorship. Also, it should be understood, voting is by occupational units, and peasants are so gerrymandered that it takes five times as many peasants as it does of proletarians to make up a unit of representation. The elections are held under the supervision of Soviet inspectors—spies. The Party slate designated at headquarters is submitted to a vote by the counting of hands, so that each voter's choice is publicly known. Failure to vote for the hand-picked nominees can result in the loss of employment. In this connection we should consider the consequences to a person of losing his job for failure to vote in accordance with the dictator's wishes, in a country where the doctrine that "all citizens should become hired employees of the State" has already practically become a reality! The democratic processes of the ballot are distorted into a delusion, and the delusion is preserved only to deceive the people of Russia and of the world into imagining that the Government has a popular mandate.

The local Soviet, the representatives of which are elected as above explained, then elects delegates to the next higher Soviet; this, to the next higher; and so forth, until delegates are finally elected to The All-Russian Soviet Congress.

The All-Russian Soviet Congress is essentially an administrative body which simply helps Stalin to decide *how* he will do what he has already decided to do.

Rosa Luxemburg, a leader of the German Communists, who was thoroughly in sympathy with the objectives of the Russian Communists, said, a few months after the Communist party came into power, describing the methods of the Soviet system:

"In the place of the representative bodies chosen by the vote of the people throughout the country Lenin and Trotsky have made the Soviets the only real representatives of the working masses. But the inevitable result of stifling the political life of the whole nation is that life in the Soviets themselves becomes gradually paralyzed. Without general elections, the unhampered freedom of the Press and liberty of speech, the life of every public institution is extinguished; it degenerates into a mere appearance of life, in which the bureaucracy is the only active element. This is a law from which there is no escape. Little by little public life becomes somnolent; a score or so of party leaders, endowed with inexhaustible energy and unlimited idealism, direct the government; and even among them the guidance of affairs is really in the hands of a round dozen men of outstanding intellect, and a few chosen members of the working classes are from time to time summoned to a meeting in order to applaud the speeches of the leaders and pass a unanimous vote in favor of the resolutions put before them. Thus it is at bottom a government by a clique—a dictatorship, it is true, but not the dictatorship of the proletariat. It is the dictatorship of a handful of politicians—that is to say, a dictatorship in the bourgeois acceptance of the term, similar to the rule of the Jacobins. . . . And, furthermore, such a state of affairs necessarily leads to a growth of brutality in public life, to assassinations, to the shootings of hostages, etc."

Her prophecy proved an understatement of fact. Complete political despotism has resulted. No vestige of political liberty remains, and this political despotism has been used as the effective instrument to impose economic slavery on the people. All property is collectivized: all industry controlled.

To insure the continuance of this political and economic system, education is also absolutely regimented. Man must be reduced to intellectual slavery to be kept in political bondage. Every idea and ideal not in accord with, and promotive of, Sovietism must be blotted from the mind of man.

And finally, religion must be, and is being, destroyed. This last challenge to the State's supremacy must be removed. The Supreme State cannot admit of any higher allegiance. Man must be accountable to the State alone.

They have thrown the gods out of heaven, but on earth Stalin is greeted by bowing delegates with the salutation: "We greet in thy person the valiant leader of the world proletariat." Here the word "thy" is significant. Under the Czar, only God and the Czar were addressed as "thou." Stalin is Czar; more than that—he is the vicar of Lenin, the Messiah of Materialism.

Today there are no human rights in Russia. In 1917 the Communists were promising liberty and peace. They were protesting against capital punishment, saying "The life of workers and peasants must be held sacred and inviolate." Their dictatorship was to be "transitory." In Danton's words (he was speaking of the revolutionary committees in the French Revolution): "the object was to establish a sort of dictatorship of those citizens who were most whole-heartedly devoted to liberty for the purpose of keeping in subjection those who had become suspect." Alas for those who tamper with principles *temporarily!* "Power always corrupts, and absolute power corrupts absolutely . . ." and now a Soviet journalist writing of human beings can say: "Of these *goods* we have plenty."

Sovietism is, indeed, the fanatical extreme of the

New Despotisms but it well pictures what actually develops from the doctrine of a government of men, not laws.

D. KAMALISM

The Turkish dictatorship under Kamal Ataturk, who, as Mustafa Kamal Pasha, head of his country's armed forces, won a smashing victory where defeat seemed certain, and, consequently, established the present regime, in 1922, is nearer to the Nazi ideal than to Mussolini's, because Kamalism is informed with a profound, a fanatical, belief in the racial superiority of the Turks. Kamalism is as hostile to religion as is Sovietism, and has dealt with racial minorities—Greeks, Kurds, and Armenians—as cruelly, and even more cruelly, than the Nazis with the Jews. Like the Soviets, Kamalism has an enormous admiration for the mechanical achievements of Western Civilization, but wants none of its democracy. Kamalism is not only the most successful, but also the most primitive of all the dictatorships. It is a complete tribal tyranny. It is also the most Oriental. The older traditions of its people are farthest from Western thought; and it is for this reason that practically all our comparisons are made with the two despotisms of Western Europe, Fascism and Nazism, and with Sovietism. Mention, however, had to be made of this New Despotism because it is also contributing to the world movements toward these new isms; and more especially because many observers see a growing tendency in Russia toward this type of dictatorship. No further mention of it, however, need be made, in the subsequent chapters of this book.

The regimes of Mussolini, Hitler, Stalin, and Kamal are all merely different versions of the same "new" political theory. Under the pretense of serving the greatest good of the greatest number, they all have concentrated absolute political power in one individual. They are by intention permanent absolutisms: simple, primitive, tyrannies; with their power over the lives, minds, souls, and bodies of their subjects, at least in theory, if not also in practice, unchecked and unrestrained by any written constitution, by living tradition, or by any power except the arbitrary will of a man. Their modes of thinking, their strategy, and their ambitions, are the same. In their economic theories, into which our theme does not carry us, they differ; but politically, in their hatred of Nineteenth Century Liberalism, and in their contempt for the ideals of democracy and for civil liberties, they are unanimous. They are fanatics in their hostility to religion—though Mussolini and

Hitler have had to make compromises—because if man has faith in some divinity, he has thereby a belief in laws, in values that are eternal and supreme, and which contradict the dogmas of the dictator's omniscience and omnipotence. Religion is, in their opinion, a barrier in the way of the perfect fulfillment of the totalitarian idea. The Totalitarian State destroys our spiritual values. It sacrifices man to the political and economic processes. Indeed, there is a tendency in all the totalitarian countries even to deify the dictator.

Another common characteristic of all these dictators is their impassioned emphasis on nationalistic and racial pride and prejudices. They also strive to consolidate their power by building up in the minds of their people the bugaboo of danger from other nations. They thereby seek to divert attention at home from their own maneuvers, and to solidify themselves in their usurpations, under the pretext of taking so much power only to meet the challenge of the common foe. They cultivate animosities in the minds and hearts of their people against particular nations which they single out as blocking the achievement of their national destiny and of their getting their "place in the sun." Also they become obsessed with the religious urge to propagate their faith and to save humanity by imposing their culture on the "uncivilized." They are all a constant threat to international peace. As President Roosevelt rightfully observes: "Peace is threatened by those who seek selfish power." ". . . autocracy in world affairs endangers peace and that such threats do not spring from those nations devoted to the democratic ideal."

These modern despotisms are "a return to the primitive before the conception of impersonal law was born." They are not a bold step forward, but are more like a collapse backward into the past. They are purely reversions to the old tyrannies. These old notions are resurrected from the dark past to illuminate, or better, to blind, the present.

It is well to weigh in our hearts and minds the words of Matteotti, the Italian, who said in Brussels shortly before he met his death for opposing Mussolini:

"Liberty is like the air and the sun. One has to be deprived of them before one knows that one cannot live without them."

Let us proceed now to inform ourselves of the basic ideas and ideals of some of the official expositors of the New Deal—the Minor Prophets of the New Order —as they themselves explain these and strive to put them into practice, so that we may thus learn the direction and discern the goal of their political thinking, and be in this manner forewarned of the danger these Prophets are bringing to the Constitution and to our liberties, by the similarity of the doctrines they are preaching, the objectives they are advocating, and the methods they are trying to use, to the theories and the practices—as we studied them in this Chapter—of the New Despotisms.

CHAPTER VI

SOME MINOR PROPHETS

AMERICANISM and the New Despotisms are the antipodes of political philosophy. It is impossible to conceive of two systems more contradictory.

Under Americanism, Man is divinely endowed with natural rights, and is historically possessed of civil liberties, both of which are recognized as inalienable, and are safeguarded, in a written constitutional guarantee, as unassailable by government; the State is the creature of Man; it is the convenient political mechanism designed and constituted to further the enjoyment of individual freedom in an orderly civil society; it has only those prerogatives and functions which its sovereign citizens from time to time expressly grant it; it is a means to an end; it is a government of laws, not of men; and law emanates from reason and from the sovereign people.

Under the New Despotisms, Man is the mere creature of the State, and has only those rights which are voluntarily granted him by the State, and his enjoyment of them is a mere revocable license from the State; the State is an end in itself: man is a mere "means"; the State is omniscient and omnipotent; it is a government of men, not of laws; and all law emanates from the arbitrary will of the dominating group or individual.

These two theories of government are obviously basically incompatible. They will not, and cannot, be mixed. The slightest compromise with the primal principles of Americanism, even the most casual and temporary departure therefrom, removes the only anchorage which can hold the State steadfast in its obedience to the people, and sets it adrift on the tide that sweeps toward the totalitarian idea.

We must, of course, assume social responsibilities in the exercise of our individual liberties. Membership in any society requires the acceptance of social obligations, and demands that the community interests be consulted and promoted. Individual liberty can be perfectly enjoyed only in a land of liberty, but it has not been historically demonstrated that the public welfare can be served in any desirable way by the complete obliteration of individual freedom and the absolute absorption of the individual by the State. On the contrary, that procedure inevitably leads to the destruction of all liberty, social as well as individual. The promotion of the general well-being does not require that we surrender our all to the unrestrained opinion of a transient majority or to the absolute benevolence of a single individual. Principles, not men, must be the criteria of political as well as of individual behavior.

Now, we are *not* suggesting that Americanism has already been transformed into totalitarianism. We are only attempting to understand the basic principles of the philosophies of these two diametrically opposed systems and then to read recent political trends or tendencies in the United States in their respective lights. Political transformation have always been initiated by a "new" direction, or orientation, in political thinking.

It is highly important, therefore, that we seek to understand even the obscure implications in the teachings of some of those Minor Prophets of the "New Order," to whom circumstances have given positions from which they can exercise a directive influence. We will not intentionally over-emphasize the similarities between their spoken words and those of the leaders of the New Despotisms; much less call into question their sincerity or good intentions. Undoubtedly their plans, so far as they can see, are for the general welfare of mankind: their goal seems to them glorious.

They are militant crusaders against the abuses and defects in our existing system—and of abuses and defects there are glaring and proven examples. But to repair the consequences and to prevent the reoccurence of these regrettable instances, it is not necessary to destroy our institutions; at least, it has not as yet been demonstrated that reform, recognized as necessary, cannot be secured by measures wholly *within* the provisions of our Constitution. We challenge the claim that these evident evils are a necessary concomitant of our institutions, and maintain that these evils arise solely from the abuse, not the use, of our institutions.

In the question of departures from our fundamental principles of government, we do not differentiate between deviations which are to the Right and those which are to the Left: it is with the "departures" themselves that we quarrel; it is these we fear.

We note among all the Minor Prophets similarities in historical theory, in political attitudes. One has contempt for the "horse-and-buggy age," another, for the "liberal" nineteenth century, both meaning the period ending with their accession. More important politically, foreign dictators and these American "democrats"—obviously their imitators—excel in the subtle game of inventing new kinds of liberty, or rather substitutes for liberty. We must not be deceived by the dialectic of either the foreign dictator or of our own "New Democrats." We must study and weigh the real content of the words of our Minor Prophets. Words with a soft sound, a mild connotation, have been uniformly employed by all the authors of the "new freedom" painlessly to introduce the more severe actuality of their ideas. Let us now permit a few of these minor prophets to speak for themselves, so as not, even inadvertently, to do any of them the injustice of putting inexact words into their mouths!

Mr. Donald R. Richberg, former Administrator of the N.R.A., in his address at Rutgers University, March 28, 1935, said:

"If the system of private enterprise is to be preserved it should be abundantly clear that the excesses of competition and the excesses of profit-making must be prevented by social discipline."

Mussolini in his speech on Capitalism and the Corporative State, November, 1933, gives us the true significance of "social discipline"; he said:

"Today we bury economic liberalism. . . . Corporationism is disciplined economy, and from that comes control, because one cannot imagine a discipline without a director. Corporationism is above socialism and above liberalism. . . ."

Rex G. Tugwell, in his speech before the Rochester Teachers' Association, April 9, 1935, however, used different words to describe the same basic idea.

"Prophecy is always dangerous and I shall not attempt to prophesy the changes in our social and economic life which might come as a result of utilizing the present program of relief for the cultivation of this Third Economic system. Yet it is altogether possible that this system will be the means by which we reconcile and assign the respective spheres of what we call socialism and what we call individualism."

What fundamental difference in economic substance and effect is there between Richberg's "social discipline" and Tugwell's "Third Economy," or between either of these and Mussolini's "Corporationism?" Are they not all, in purpose at least, the same thing?

The "social discipline" of the New Dealers must not be confused with the authority the government exercises only as police power to insure the successful working of our constitutional processes, and to assure the enjoyment of individual liberty free from all encroachments, political or economic. The punishment of abuses of, and the protection of the public interest in, the conduct of private enterprise, as is provided in such legislation as the so-called "Antitrust Laws," the Clayton Act, the Federal Trade Commission Act, and others of like character, have totally different objectives and certainly a more restricted scope. Social discipline as it is preached by the Minor Prophets means industrial regimentation —the complete subordination of private enterprise to the State's dictates. Not as yet has it been extended to the denial of the right for the title to property to be vested in private persons, but only to the absolute control over its use. Its champions seek to supersede an economy of free enterprise, a competitive capitalism, by a socialized state of planned and controlled enterprise. They seek not only to perfect the present economic system, but also to set up a new economic order. In this respect, "social discipline" resembles Fascism in some aspects and Nazism in others, both of which admit the principle of private ownership of property but subordinate its use to the program of the State. Sovietism, of course, denies private ownership and collectivizes all property in a theoretically communistic State.

We need no further proof as to what is possible under Mr. Richberg's mild term "social discipline" than to note the practical application of "social discipline" under the N.R.A. There was a telling difference between the textual content of the National Industrial Recovery Act and its actual administration, which well illustrated the inclination of those vested with its enforcement. We were there given a very illuminating example of "social discipline" in its workings according to their designs.

Mr. Tugwell, in his speech before the Rochester Teachers' Association, "explores the geography of what could be called the Third Economy—the sphere which belongs neither to private profit nor State

Socialism. . . ." He argues that the sacred duty "in the discharge of which the individual may be required to lay down his life and until recently his fortune as well" in the defense of his country in war should be continued through times of peace. This doctrine of emergency justification for transgression against our constitutional institutions found quite general advocacy here as it did in the inauguration of all of the New Despotisms in Europe. It is a patriotic appeal to surrender our freedom for the general welfare—as general welfare is conceived by a power-seeking group.

Dr. Tugwell explains that "for at least a century in this country we have recognized the value both to private profit and to State solvency of purely public and non-profitable enterprises such as good roads and safe bridges"; the post office, "streets, water systems, community sanitation and recreation grounds have gradually ceased to be private and become public." To these the present Administration has added "certain categories of public works, which being designed to preserve and develop broadly generalized economic values, cannot return direct profit to the State or to the individual." He illustrates such categories as including the prevention of "soil erosion, by dams, by drainage canals, by cover-crops, shelter-belts, reforestation and afforestation, drainage, flood and wind control." Impelled by this line of thinking, he continues on his merry way to add: "our land utilization policy, taken in conjunction with projects for rural housing, rural sanitation, rural electrification, self-help industries," and "recreational facilities, educational, artistic and cultural enterprises."

His vision of his "Third Economy" does not stop there! He is driven on by the irresistible force of his own logic, but is cautious to select words of mild meaning so as not too suddenly and severely to shock our established beliefs. But his direction and the ultimate destination of his proposals seem clear! Here is how he explains them himself:

"For the main task of production we shall always have to work under some *form of coordination,* whether that coordination is expressed through public control over hours, wages, prices and conditions of employment, or through what President Roosevelt has called partnership with industry. Coordination is the essential element in large scale production, whether it be production of kilowatt hours under a utilities holding company or the production of wheat and cotton under the Triple-A, or the old production for the vanished market of Adam Smith and the conventional economist. *It seems to me that we are now engaged in a more or less conscious process of reassigning and redistributing powers and controls in this indispensable co-*

ordination. In certain spheres, no doubt, where enterprise is affected with a public interest we shall be forced to resort to an increasing degree of public authority to achieve the necessary control. Public ownership of certain utilities seems to me clearly forecast by present facts. . . . All that we can be certain of is the fact that through banking, through such cooperative enterprises as N.R.A. or through the device of private management companies, some effective coordination of large-scale production will be necessary. In that respect, the only true question is whether bankers, businessmen or politicians—each responsible to different constituencies—shall be the coordinators." (Italics ours.)

We venture to comment at this point that "coordination" under the N.R.A., did not prove to be President Roosevelt's "partnership with industry," but rather to be a government by compulsion. It was not voluntary, but was "social discipline" imposed by government. Tugwell seems very clearly to understand the real import of Roosevelt's words as "coordination" under the N.R.A. was in fact a "form of coordination" "expressed through public control."

Tugwell then boldly asserts that "we are now engaged in a more or less conscious process of reassigning and redistributing powers and controls," and that "we shall be forced to resort to an increasing degree of public authority to achieve the necessary control."

How strange it seems to us for him to speak of "reassigning and redistributing powers," and resorting to public authority to "achieve the necessary control," in a land where governmental powers are constitutionally assigned and distributed, and in which "public authority" means constitutional authority and the limits of that authority have been defined and the purposes of their use stipulated! Were these powers constitutionally designed and intended to create implements of "control?"

Certainly it is pertinent for us at this juncture to ask ourselves the following questions: Does Dr. Tugwell mean to suggest that "spheres" of enterprise which are "affected with a public interest" are those which can be expanded and elaborated to fit the social and economic theories and designs of any particular group of men at any one time composing the government? What are the limitations, if any, of these "spheres?" Can any enterprise by mere legislative declaration or executive fiat be included in these "spheres?" We here note a foreshadowing of President Roosevelt's "rounded whole."

The subtlety of Dr. Tugwell's reasoning is striking and so too are all its potentialities, particularly when he does not hesitate to say that we are engaged "in a more or less conscious progress." Dr. Tugwell is certainly "conscious"; the people perhaps much less so, that this "Third Economy" means an entirely new social and economic order. It is indeed an ambitious undertaking!

But Dr. Tugwell's speech before the Democratic State Central Committee of California on October 28, 1935 is probably the most startling and challenging discourse thus far made by anyone having a responsible official position and enjoying such great presidential favor; it is wholly enlightening as to the mind of Dr. Tugwell and his colleagues. Of course, Dr. Tugwell is the boldest, the most outspoken, of all the Minor Prophets, and has possibly progressed much further than many of the others; but, not only has he not been repudiated by his master or associates, but he seems to have been peculiarly prophetic in forecasting Administration policies and activities. His newspaper interview, given after the 1932 election but before inauguration, proved to be more accurately the Administration's program than was the Democratic Party's platform adopted at the Chicago Convention. Dr. Tugwell is the psychoanalyst of the New Deal.

In this California speech we have one beautiful example after another of that nice substitution of the more familiar, gentler, American designation for the corresponding harsh unattractive words used by the dictators of the New Despotisms, but these words in principle and substance have exactly the same meaning: to illustrate with a few examples, "Hate" becomes "indignation," "obedience" becomes "democratic discipline," "revolutionary" becomes "progressive." This speech is spoken in the mood of Mussolini just before the March on Rome, of the Bolsheviki in 1917, and of Hitler a half dozen years ago. Let us read from it carefully and ask ourselves what is likely to be the next step of men who are thinking these things *now?* It reads like an oration over the grave of the despised nineteenth century liberalism—an announcement of the New State based on the "Third Economy."

But let Dr. Tugwell again speak for himself; and this time at considerable length:

"How deep are the sources of your indignation? Do they lie on the surface and are they at the command of those who would have you turn against a national government which has invaded the modern strongholds of privilege? Or do they lie deeper so that your wrath may sustain a genuine reconstruction of American life?

"For the sickness of our system is not yet cured. We have made some diagnoses; we have got some partial remedies; we have made a good beginning. That it is not yet enough must be admitted—we still have the testimony of poverty, debt and unemployment; but, with what it is, we shall soon be required to ask for a new mandate. And what is needed in these months to come is an access of confidence among all progressives, a submission to discipline under leadership, and a drive for complete victory against the most powerful reaction ever organized in this nation. If we cannot achieve unity we shall lose—and we shall deserve to lose. For this time we have the fact of accomplishment behind us and a leader who deserves our loyalty; discipline is the only lack.

"What I have to say to you, therefore, is of this sort; we must draw together, nursing the sources of that anger which has driven us forward and making more and more clear the great hopes which pull us in the same direction.

"What we are witnessing now is the death struggle of industrial autocracy and the birth of democratic discipline. . . .

"We have no reason to expect that the disestablishment of our plutocracy will be pleasant. These historical changes never are. We have, however, the duty of avoiding violence as the process goes on. And this is why I regard the coming months as among the critical ones of our history. . . .

"There will be no end to his (man's) advances so long as the urges within him remain unimpaired; but it will be multiplied a thousand-fold once he gives up the sterile morality of individualism. . . . But we do need a clearer and wider recognition of the main trends we are in and a straightforward movement to claim their advantages. If this requires the removal of barriers, that is historically unimportant. We need only care as human beings how it is done. The autocrats must get out of the way along with the moral system which supports them; but it is our duty to prevent that being done with violence. That is why I regard the coming campaign as so important. *It may very well determine whether, some years from now, we shall do as other nations have—throw over completely the democratic and evolutionary process— or whether we shall find then that our leadership, our administration and our discipline have been equal to the task of creating institutions suited to the world in which they are expected to operate.* Reaction at this time would commit us to a future uncertain in many ways, but certain enough in this; that there would be a vast rising of rebellious, exploited people after we had revived for a while the game of getting rich at one another's expense. . . .

"The whole record . . . is a progressive one. . . . It is a record on which we are entitled to unity. . . . We must make certain that all of our friends are with us and that all of our enemies are against us—and one is about as essential as the other. A progressive political army marches on its morale—and the sources of our morale are two; enthusiasm for a challenging national task well begun and the existence of an enemy we can despise with a lasting and righteous anger." (Italics ours.)

Having boasted at length that the "parity principle," as applied by the Administration, has worked wonders for the relief of agriculture, Tugwell strongly urges that "it is all important that farmers and workers should see how their interests merge in the parity principle, how the interests of one can be made the interest of all." His Russian experiences seem to have associated farmers and industrial workers in his mind as the natural combination to bring about the new social and economic order. He, however, anticipates difficulty in importing this Russian communistic conception to this country and wedding it to the "parity principle" in industry, as he says:

". . . I have the feeling also that the compulsion needed for industrial change is more likely to come from the workers than from present owners. So many of the owners stand to gain from disorder and disunity rather than from cooperation that united action for such a purpose seems remote and unlikely. It is the workers who stand to gain most—just as the dirt-farmer stands to gain most in agriculture. These, as I have said, are our natural progressive allies in the days of change which are now upon us. And so, we come back to the question of strategy. The farmers and the workers must not permit themselves to be separated. Theirs is a common cause. And hope and confidence ought to flow from the obvious gains to be got from its forthright recognition."

Dr. Tugwell sums up with this dramatic statement: *"We must make irrevocable political commitment to disciplined democracy, to calculated change of institutions whenever that may be necessary, so that they may insure the expression of our national aims."* (Italics ours.)

Careful consideration of these lengthy quotations from the utterances of the crusading doctor makes it manifest that constitutional limitations give Dr. Tugwell no great concern. He boasts: "Serious legal difficulties which have been interposed against these reforms we have refused to regard as insuperable."

When Dr. Tugwell uses the adjective "progressive" it has a distinct Marxian flavor. He says: "My Progressive colleagues frequently say that what we need is a Plan—a Plan with a capital P which should outline in detail and with limits of time the goals to be sought and achieved for the nation." This Plan he gives them. "We have established a record now which may well substitute itself for the plan and the minority dictatorship which others use." This is an amazing statement. Dr. Tugwell tells his colleagues that they do not need the "Plan," which they seek, as they already have such a "Plan" in the record they have established. This record is not only a "Plan," according to Dr. Tugwell, but is a susbstitute for the "minority dictatorship which others use." Obviously, he must mean the Soviets, as they are the only ones who have published such a plan with a capital "P."

This Plan, or record, as Dr. Tugwell prefers to designate it,—the "Third Economy"—has a very decided fascist orientation, and is basically inharmonious with our constitutional concepts and dialectic. Mussolini speaks of "liberalism, socialism, and corporationism," the latter being "above" the first two; Dr. Tugwell, of "socialism, individualism, and the Third Economy," the latter to "reconcile" the first two. Furthermore the record thus far established speaks for itself and discloses the consummation of much of the "Plan."

Mr. Richberg, another expositor of the Plan, has some interesting observations to make. In his address at Knox College, June 13, 1935, he said that the Constitution of a political government must provide for the development and the maintenance of the Constitution of an economic government, or the political Constitution will "prove to be a mockery and a delusion." He further said that the workers, once slaves to liege lords were, now, in the machine age, tending day by day toward "involuntary dependence" on the irresponsible controllers of an economic system.

"Experimentation" was necessary, Richberg contends, to meet the new trend. Thus he adumbrates what might well be called "The Richberg Governmental Experimentation Laboratory." "We need for the guidance of future public policies the work of the pure scientist who is content to be one of the noble company who seek to reveal only the truth." And to these experts "legislative and judicial bodies should accord the authority now yielded to the physician and the chemist." The suggestion that the body politic is to be subjected to laboratory experiments, free from any control except the scientific fancy of political experimenters; and that legislative bodies heretofore accountable to the people, and judicial bodies responsible to the "Supreme law of the land," should in the future "accord the authority now yielded to the physician and the chemist" to these pure scientists, must have been advanced in jest, as a satire on all political scientists; otherwise it is a fanciful idea beyond our understanding.

Now, this is all either verbal nonsense or it has deep implications. Our Federal Government was, as has been said, designed and constituted as a political instrumentality effectively to carry out its limited and defined mission. It was the plan of the political State, not the "Plan" for an economic order of society. The citizen was intended to be free to work out his own economic destiny, not to have his economic activities and social life prescribed and controlled by the State. Our political system was intended to give him economic freedom, economic independence, not to subject him to absolute dependence on the State. Every unnecessary interference of government with the freedom of individual industry was considered by our ancestors as a check on individual effort and personal liberty.

What is this "Constitution of an economic government" which Mr. Richberg thinks so essential? We would very much like to inspect its entire content before we adopt it. The skeletonized outline disclosed by the teachings of the Minor Prophets and by recent legislation gives us, however, some idea of its general objectives and methods, and we note many similarities with the initial steps taken in establishing the New Despotisms. Their sponsors propose political despotism as the only means to free man from what they call "economic autocracy." Personally, we have equal contempt for, and fear of, both.

It needs no argument to prove that some reform is imperative, for to deny that reform is necessary is to suggest the absurdity that perfection has already been attained, and to close one's eyes as well to many glaring examples of its need. Reform must, however, be distinguished from Revolution. Reform is the correction of abuses, the prevention of their recurrence, the adaptation of the existing State to changed conditions; it is not the discarding of the existing

order and the susbstituting of a different system. It
is the objective sought which supplies the cest of the
social value of the effort, but we must be careful, that
in our enthusiasm to attain this objective, and in our
righteous indignation against abuses, we do not even
unconsciously select and pursue methods which alter
all our accepted concepts of government.

Nor has it yet been demonstrated by the New
Dealers, or by anybody else, that our political institutions are substantially outmoded, that malpractices
and abuses cannot be corrected, and that all adjust-
ments needed to square them with progress, cannot
be made within the framework of our institutions.
Moreover, we need not look far to see that the ultimate fulfillment of the "reforms" which are being
proposed leads to a system even more tyrannous and
class-privileged than that which these Minor Prophets
claim the present system to be.

It is obvious that a studied attempt is being made
not only to utilize the Federal Government as an
agency for social service in meeting emergency conditions, but also permanently to expand the Federal
Government's functions so as to make social service
part of the Government's mission. This goes far
beyond the earlier limited concept that the government is primarily a political instrumentality. But
this is not all. The permanent social service is but
a first step. From the confessed ideals of these cru-

saders it is apparent that they seek to profit by the present economic emergency to set up a permanent new order—the "Third Economy," perhaps,—and it is with the fundamental concepts of that "Constitution of an economic government" that they are concerned.

Mr. Richberg, in his speech at Rutgers University, March 28, 1935, on "Reconstructed Individualism," said: "The particular forms of individual freedom which distinguished our pioneer civilization have disappeared. . . ." He says a "new discipline" is necessary to meet the requirements of modern life, and then declares:

"This freedom which we all crave must be gathered today—not by letting people alone—but by making sure that they are so organized for cooperation that the continuous interchange of necessary products and services will not break down. . . ."

We assume that by the "forms of individual freedom" of "our pioneer civilization," he means our constitutional institutions of individual freedom and self-government, as these were established by our Founding Fathers. He can have no other meaning as that is the only form of individual freedom that we have as yet sought to establish. If that has "disappeared," as he says, then he is even more daring in his accusation than we are, for we have only suggested that those "forms of individual freedom" were being threatened and destroyed by the New Dealers, but not that they had already "disappeared."

Dr. Tugwell, the schoolman, and Mr. Richberg, the jurist, have been the intellectual expositors, the scientific formulators, of these new political conceptions, and have been the technicians of the "Third Economy." Henry Wallace, on the other hand, is the mystic prophet. He contributes its mythology, its ideality; he adds its beatific vision; he impregnates it with, and gives it, the impetus of a religious fervor. It is an interesting coincidence that his middle name "Agard" so closely approximates "Asgard," which is the paradise of ancient Nordic mythology. Wallace best reveals his philosophy in his recent book "New Frontiers," the apocalypse of the New Deal. His frontiers are mystical, not geographical. They are the outlines of the "new" human nature, transformed; of a "social discipline," an "economic democracy." This new order, though he does not pick his colleague's words, is, evidently, the "Third Economy" of Dr. Tugwell.

There is, certainly, a strangely revealing similarity in the selection of the names with which both Tugwell and Wallace designate their reciprocally interlocking political faiths. This similarity in the nomenclature of the intellectual expositor and of the mystic prophet of the New Deal in America betrays a startling likeness, not only in their own mental processes, but also with the workings of the minds of the masters and prophets of the New Despotisms in Europe. There is, for instance, the Third International of Tovaritch Stalin; the Third Reich of Herr Hitler; the tripartite nature of Signor Mussolini's Corporationism; and the Third Economy of Dr. Tugwell. The number "three" seems to have a strange fascination, a magical charm and import, for all these utopians.

They all seem also to be impressed with the use of symbols as an effective means of appealing to the popular eye. Mussolini uses the old Roman fasces to recall the majesty and the imperial grandeur and power of Rome; Stalin, the crossed sickle and hammer to depict the concerted interest and action of the farmer and the industrial laborer; and Hitler, the swastika, the emblem of promise of good fortune.

Henry Wallace has adopted a mystical symbol for his creed—three spheres within a larger circle— an ancient symbol, which like Hitler's swastika is of Oriental origin. Mr. Wallace uses this symbol in his book, and describes it as follows:

"From the standpoint of guiding principles for the future, there is a design drawn from the far past which seems to be appropriate, because it suggests the maximum development of individual diversity within the limitations of the whole. Medieval painters used to put it in one corner of their work. It is the design used by Nicholas Roerich for the Banner of Peace and incorporated in the Roerich Pact for the protection of cultural treasures. The design represents three spheres—symbolic of the Trinity, within a larger circle. The circle of course represents the idea of unity. With its universal application it is not surprising that this symbol has been used in all ages—one may find it perhaps, upon a Christ of Memling, an Ikon of St. Sergius, or Tibetan banner. This design has great depths of meaning in this infinitely more complex world of today. The uniqueness of each individual and each community must be realized but always (instinctively, by the necessity of inner compulsion) with reference to the national and world community. All individuals, classes and nations which approach the future with beauty of spirit might well unite their economic, social and cultural endeavors within this imagined circle of unifying freedom. . . ."

And so the New Deal, translated into the "Third Economy" by its official philosopher, has been well symbolized by its official mystic.

Wallace himself says that in his "New Frontiers" he has "tried to condense into broad material objectives the philosophy of the New Deal," and he certainly is not without official credentials to speak for the New Deal. Let us, therefore, linger for a few

**TRIPARTITE
CORPORATIONISM**
Fascism

THIRD REICH
Nazism

THIRD INTERNATIONALE
Sovietism

THIRD ECONOMY
New Dealism

minutes in his three-ringed utopia, examining its ideas and cautiously discerning its words. We may profitably begin with this sentence:

"It is our privilege and disadvantage to look at the Bourbons, the wealthy troglodytes of the preceding generation, repeating in their ignorance outworn phrases, seeking to patch their outworn economic structure."

Here, undoubtedly, "outworn economic structure" means trade, industry for profit; human ambition; the motives and methods which we meet on every page of human history: "outworn phrases," probably, analogously mean tradition, historical continuity, and the acceptance of tested and proven facts.

Wallace thus allegorically expresses another of his fanciful ideas:

"My generation wishes the new generation would spend more time trying to build seaworthy vessels in which to reach a new world and less time bothering with the troglodytes, who are rapidly dying off, anyway."

In other words, the "enemy class" is being, as Stalin would vulgarly express it, "liquidated."

"All of us under sixty years of age," in Wallace's words, "are desperately in need of some means of conveyance to this new world." This must mean that we are seeking "new instruments of public power" to transport us to a society organized into the "Third Economy" where not liberty, but "democratic discipline," would be the enjoyment of the citizenry.

Persistently faithful to his allegory, Wallace continues to take the world into his confidence:

"Few past fifty like to think of building such vessels. That is left for youth. I think the youth of America is about ready to try it. And there are some gray-heads among them."

Wallace tells us that these New Deal vessels are destined on "a journey toward frontiers quite different from any we have ever known in the United States." Evidently, therefore these frontiers must lie beyond the boundaries of our present constitutional limitations.

He further elucidates: "We must invent, build and put to work new social machinery. This machinery will carry out the Sermon on the Mount as well as the present social machinery carries out and intensifies the law of the jungle."

Man, in a word, is going to be perfected by a "social invention," by politics, which, as Wallace promises, will bring about "vast but possible changes . . . in human hearts and minds. . . ."

He continues: "To a social inventor definite human responses to new rules of the game, in American commerce and agriculture, are as important as were the existing laws of physics and mechanics to the first automotive inventors"; and a little further on, still continuing this naive exposure of a dreamer's simplification of ideas and truths: "a mathematical realization that in a world such as ours, short-time, local, selfish solutions merely create confusion. . . ."

"I am hoping," says Wallace, not very hopefully, "that we can advance by means of an aroused, educated Democracy. Socialism, Communism, and Fascism, it is true, have the advantage of certain precise rules not available to Democracy. They make the path to the land of tomorrow seem straight and short. The only rules a democracy can rely upon make the path seem by comparison long and tortuous."

The objective of Fascism and Communism is, evidently, also the objective of Mr. Wallace's three-ringed utopia as he reveals in these words:

"In our march to a real democracy, governmental powers should not be loaned too lightly to any group. For the ultimate security of that loan, there must be clear-cut evidence that the power will be used to advance a harmonious relationship between forces now contending. The degree to which this principle can be grasped and applied by businessmen, laborers, and farmers reared in a freebooter tradition remains to be seen. That, as it develops, will set the practical limits of 'self-governing industry' and 'self-governing agriculture.' "

The "freebooter tradition" must be Wallace's polite designation for Signor Mussolini's "more or less decomposed body of the Goddess of Liberty."

Wallace continues: "In the Democracy of tomorrow the people will have to be so intelligently free from prejudice that neither the wealthy, interested in private control or control for personal ends, nor demagogues interested in their jobs, will be able to create deception and illusion."

"If we are not to go in for Communism or Fascism, it is essential that government learn to look on itself as a partner with business, labor, agriculture and consumers."

To avoid disaster according to Wallace's idea: "it will be necessary to get more and more of our people thinking seriously about that continuously balanced harmonious relationship which I call the Land of Tomorrow." He goes on to say that if the industries "dodge" their responsibility for the unemployed— (a responsibility computed by whom?) then it "will be the duty of the Government to go ahead with its own method of rehabilitation and build out of the unemployed a self-subsistence system of exchange cooperatives which are outside the capitalistic system."

He thus gives a complete picture of a centralized government directing industry, farming, and the lives of all its people; in short that is his three-ringed utopia.

"New freedoms and new deals nearly always cost millions of dollars." "But the greatest cost is the social discipline required to bring new ways of looking at things."

Wallace here naively confesses that the cost of his "new deals" cannot be measured only by millions of dollars, but even in a greater measure by the sacrifice of personal liberties through "social discipline."

Then he heaves this chunk of wisdom at our devoted heads:

"There has to be, first of all, a mechanism; and above all, there has to be a discipline sufficient to keep the mechanism in motion." Why, three million farmers have just been getting lessons from Dr. Wallace in "economic self-government" and "their social discipline was equal to" a million obstacles! "They did discover how to modify individual behavior in the common good." At least, Wallace has here so assured us. Hopefully he declares:

"There can be a rebirth of genuine democracy, and there can flow from it whatever social discipline the future requires."

"Social discipline," governmental control and regimentation—not constitutional restraints—is, apparently, the democratic process which Wallace and his followers emphasize as his governmental implement to bring about his economic millennium.

"Economic democracy must be in a position to resist unwise political pressure."

Mr. Wallace must here mean that his utopian state to be successful must be so endowed by the government with power over all economic affairs, and must be so unrestrained in its exercise of this power, as to be able to ride over, or break through, any constitutional barriers or political opposition which may be interposed. In this opinion he is well informed, because it has been proven historically that no such power can be long and effectively exercised over the lives and property of people without the ruthless use of a strong instrument of discipline and compulsion. The would-be dictators of the New Deal are certainly running true to type when they advocate this strong-arm economic-political doctrine.

Obviously speaking also for his economic-political co-religionists, and more in sorrow than in anger, Wallace thus refers to the "Old Rugged Individualist": "Of necessity, they will recognize competitive individualists and competitive nations and deal with them as the anachronisms they are, treating them kindly, firmly, and carefully."

The principle of competition, in individuals and nations—the readiness with which each individual and nation seizes every opportunity of bettering his or its condition, and of advancing their individual fortune—the primary cause of production—is to be "recognized" as an "anachronism." It certainly requires unbounded confidence on Mr. Wallace's part for him to think that he can transform human nature by "social invention."

In the last line in his book,—the "New Frontiers" —he most tersely summarizes his theory of constitutional government:

"This mechanism for a concert of interest skilfully worked out should provide in considerable measure the unwritten constitution which will govern many of our most significant advances toward economic democracy."

His "mechanism" is the central government. This central government is to be omnipotent, a law unto itself, for he says that the "mechanism" "should provide in considerable measure the *unwritten constitution*" of the new "economic democracy." This is the flat repudiation of our theories of Constitutional Democracy. It is the advocacy of the underlying principle of the Totalitarian State: a government of men, not of laws. His central government is to have no written constitution, but is to be its own "unwritten constitution." His qualification "in a considerable measure" is his mild way of introducing us to this alien conception.

When we consider that these Minor Prophets, whose theories, and the methods and means of putting them into practice, we have been studying in this chapter, were officially entrusted with the administration of both the N.R.A. and the A.A.A., considered the principal pillars of the New Deal, we cannot escape the conclusion that their political theories and objectives must represent, or certainly closely approximate, the views of the Chief Executive. Furthermore, the mechanism of the N.R.A. and of the A.A.A. was conducive to the effectuating of their theories, and the respective laws setting up each of these administrations delegated to their administrators practically unlimited "instruments of public power" to impose "social discipline" on industry and on agriculture. If these laws were not born in the minds of these Minor Prophets—and a pronounced paternal resemblance is to be noted—then they were at least brought to their maturity and death under their ministrations and care. The pronunciamentos of these Prophets are not mere class-room teachings, but have been put into practice as national policies and governmental actions. Their importance, therefore, as causes inspiring the policies of the present Administration, cannot be over-emphasized. For that reason, we may profitably pursue our study of the teachings and the ideas of some more Minor Prophets of the "New Deal."

CHAPTER VII

MORE MINOR PROPHETS

THE political philosophy of the New Deal is given different descriptive titles by each of its leading expositors selecting his own pet name for his own particular brand, but the fundamental theory is always the same. We have already seen that Richberg's "social discipline," Tugwell's "Third Economy," and Wallace's "New Frontiers," all elaborate different phases and aspects of the "unwritten constitution" of what, we will see, President Roosevelt calls the "New Order" or the "Abundant Life."

There are still, however, two other Minor Prophets, Dr. Mordecai Ezekiel and Secretary Harold Ickes, who because of their high official positions in the hierarchy of "economic democracy," deserve some consideration in our efforts to get at the substance of the political thinking of the New Deal. Dr. Ezekiel and Secretary Ickes, true to type, have their own novel and favorite expressions and figures of speech with which they expound their understanding of it. We will let these Prophets think aloud, each in his own peculiarly picturesque style, so as not to lose the fine flavor of their expression and so as not to risk putting a misinterpretation on their obscure and sometimes fantastic words.

Doctor Mordecai Ezekiel presents us with a "blueprint" of the new social order in his recent book $2500 a Year." For fear that he may not be well enough known to fame, or that his credentials be questioned, we should remember, that he is one of the veterans of the "Brain Trust," an economist of the old Federal Farm Board, and is now the economic adviser to the Department of Agriculture. In his preface he gratefully acknowledges his indebtedness to his colleagues, especially to Secretary Wallace and to Dr. Tugwell, for ideas and suggestions. This preface is, however, marred somewhat by an anticlimax postscript in which he explains that the A.A.A. decision casts doubt on the constitutionality of one of his major proposals; but he adds, nevertheless, that since he is primarily concerned with what is "economically feasible," if that aspect of his proposals be sound, "lawyers and statesmen may eventually find a way."

He feels as free from the restraint of constitutional limitation as do all of his school of thought, and is equally confident that all he has to concern himself with is the economic feasibility of his plan and that then the law will make way for its consummation. All these Prophets have absolutely no conception of, or respect for, impersonal law. Law to them is purely the formalization of their will; it should be accommodated to their ambitions. They are constitutional unmoralists. In their minds, law emanates solely from the will of man, and their belief brings them into intellectual conflict with the basic principle of constitutionalism.

We will now let Dr. Ezekiel explain the specifications of his "blue-printed" society.

He establishes "$2500 a year" as the probable minimum for an average family of four to live on comfortably, and states that we do not at present produce enough to assure that minimum income for everybody. Therefore he maintains that we must expand our production and that this necessitates the reorganizing of our social system. "Automatic recovery" has failed to appear because the profit system does not work under the conditions of today, and, therefore, "unless the necessary changes in the rules can be devised, unless ways are found to create abundance through modifying the profit system, the issue may finally be drawn as between the present economy of profits and poverty on one side, and a promised economy of socialism and abundance on the other." The trend of his mind is apparent from the ease with which he associates "the present economy of profits and poverty," on the one hand, and the "promised economy of socialism and abundance," on the other.

As he elaborates his enormously detailed national "blue-print" it becomes evident that no activity of human life is to escape his regimentation.

He says that the "blue-print" "might" be worked out democratically. We presume he means that if everybody agreed to it. He envisions a central co-ordinating organization for each industry, much like the old code authority, composed of representatives of industry and of the government; then inter-industry agencies, municipal and regional organizations; and, finally, one central chamber that would "consolidate the various industrial and regional programs." He illustrates by pointing out that farming was, under the A.A.A., ready for the "blue-print" system, being the only great industry where producers and government were already prepared to plan production nationally and to put those plans into action. To get the "blue-print" plan into operation Government credit must be temporarily employed. In the first instance the plan is to be restricted to the fields of physical production, but its author foresees the need later of organized selling.

He expresses some doubt as to whether the plan can be inaugurated voluntarily, but that gives him little concern, for he says: "a voluntary blue-print would inevitably be less satisfactory than one prepared under greater governmental authority." Further along, he gives us a glimpse at this "governmental authority." "Much persuasion might be necessary to get some concerns to abandon their previous price policies . . . The Federal Government would guarantee that each concern which followed the blue-prints would be able to dispose of its planned increase in output," but, of course, such a guarantee would be given only "when the Government agencies were satisfied that the programs were properly drawn." Furthermore, he recommends that economic coercion,—"instead of the policeman's club of legal action" the "economic force of business competition"—be employed against the unwilling, by having the government itself "compete in production" and "hire workers away from private industry." He cites the T.V.A. as an illustration of such economic compulsion.

But he does not want to stop there! "It would be desirable to have the authority to impose programs where the industry was unwilling to cooperate, if such action became necessary. Such imposed programs would levy a tax on the entire recalcitrant industry, and offer adjustment contracts—drawn up without the industry's cooperation, if necessary—to concerns willing to cooperate. This would apply a powerful economic suasion in the direction of cooperation."

All and any means, he seems to think, are justifiable to achieve the goal of himself and his associates. Every "inducement" is proposed to secure "voluntary" acceptance of their theories. Governmental compulsion in every form is recommended. The true significance of "social discipline" becomes crystal clear. Moreover, we must not forget that all these compulsions have already been tried. Witness, the N.R.A., the A.A.A., and the Guffey Coal Conservation Act. The constitutionally limited powers of government are elaborated into an absolute unlimited paternalistic state with complete control concentrated in one political unit. That is the "blue-print" of their "professed objectives." Also, Dr. Ezekiel is not quite sure that his "blue-print" for the complete regimentation of all production and distribution by the Government is constitutional. However, he allays our aroused alarm by his hopeful reflection that it "might be inaugurated within the Constitution by modifying the proposal somewhat, or a constitutional amendment would be required."

Such a government, as is planned by this "blue-print," is absolutely impossible under our present Constitution, and also is not possible under any amendment which would not completely overturn our present system, destroy our basic institutions of individual rights and self-government, and set up a totalitarian state. After listening to Dr. Ezekiel, one can have little excuse for remaining in ignorance of the real objectives of the New Deal. That meaning is the complete regimentation of our lives: planned, "blue-printed," to their smallest detail; it is the relinquishment of all our liberties to a centralized, all-powerful government; and that objective is to be achieved as gradually as may be necessary through the slow wearing down of our resistance.

Dr. Ezekiel says in passing: "After all our problem is largely to put back at work trained workers we already have, using factories, resources, and equipment already available. It is a much easier problem than Russia had, of training workers, exploiting undeveloped resources, and creating the productive equipment, before she could expand output." Russia is nowhere mentioned in his book but here. It must have slipped in while his back was turned, to put it fancifully, slipped in because Russia must be on Dr. Ezekiel's mind. That sentence is like part of some discussion that has been going on, but the rest of which we did not overhear. It is the high-light which reveals the whole mass and form of some accepted truth. Its meaning is single and quite clear: the objective of Dr. Ezekiel's "blue-print" is the objective of Russia's Five Year Plan.

The theme of this book is political; it seeks to define and explain certain opposing principles of government. It is not our purpose to disprove Dr.

Ezekiel's economic or social theories. Our primary purpose is to point out that the political principles of the New Deal, as so clearly expressed by all these Minor Prophets, are not democratic, not in accord with traditional American thinking, and are in basic principle the same as those of the New Despotisms.

Another Minor Prophet has been assigned to another branch of the government which is administering some other basic activities of the New Deal. Therefore we must have some idea of his mental processes to complete our understanding of the "march of the intellect" of our political leaders. He, however, deserves no heroic treatment in the matter of his teachings, as like his prototype, he is only valiantly fighting windmills and, incidentally, contributing a little "cussin" to the more scholarly words of his colleagues.

Harold L. Ickes, in his book, "The New Democracy," makes the following two-fold statement:

"The breakdown of the old economy has forced us to consider as never before the responsibility of the Government. We know now that we must build a new social order."

In his discussion of "The Need for Planning" Secretary Ickes repeats the familiar comparison of peacetime emergency with war; and at the same time makes very clear the New Deal attitude toward the "new social order." The context leaves no doubt at all about his meaning. That new order is to be *permanent;* the loss of our liberties will not be temporary. Could anything be clearer than the following?

"The inherent right of the Government to organize and control business, industry and finance in time of war has long been unquestioned. . . . If it is sound policy to stand shoulder to shoulder under the leadership of the Federal Government when danger threatens from without, why isn't it reasonable to pool our resources for the common welfare during periods of economic stress and strain?"

But now his mind harks back to permanency again:

"What the Government has done along this line in the past has always been done secretly or apologetically. Generally speaking, such planned control as we have had in the past has represented only a temporary emergency war policy.

"With the vanishing of the physical frontier the necessity of a rational national plan has become more and more apparent. It was left to the Administration of President Roosevelt to adopt for the first time as a national policy the theory that the country as a whole, including commerce, industry and finance, ought to be developed and used for the greatest good of the greatest number. . . ." That is to say: developed, used, controlled *permanently* by the central Government! This, then, is Mr. Ickes' "New Democracy."

His rather lengthy, but very enlightening, explanation of the New Deal's understanding of Thomas Jefferson's phrase "life, liberty and the pursuit of happiness"—an understanding which, as Mr. Ickes mildly puts it, is not "exactly" what Jefferson's was, is worthy of our pausing for a moment to consider, as it strikingly reveals that some of these New Dealers cannot even think in the same idiom as our Founding Fathers; the same words have a different import to them; a Marxian connotation, perhaps.

"Life"—"It seems clear," says Mr. Ickes, "that the government undertaking to assure the 'life' of its citizens, would first of all busy itself to protect the people from diseases of various kinds. . . . Proper living conditions are an important element in the life of every individual and the Government would also have to concern itself with housing if it would protect its citizens. . . . It should be the duty of a responsible government to assure its citizens adequate food . . . during periods of involuntary unemployment and when advancing age makes it impossible for them longer to work. . . . Thus the responsibility of a government, which accepts the spirit of Jefferson's phrase, is one that guards each citizen from birth to death with varying degrees of measures of care."

"Liberty."—"Liberty can only be had by restrict-

ing liberty." The objective, he explains, is the greatest liberty for the greatest number of people; but these are rather empty words, since we know what sort of a government Mr. Ickes' desires.

"Pursuit of Happiness."—First, Mr. Ickes puts education for everyone according to his capacity; next, the Government should "provide ways whereby the talent of the youth may be devoted to the greater good of society"; and finally, the Government should "foster the fine arts. Music, the theatre, painting and sculpture. . . ." "A national orchestra, and a national opera company may some day be an integral part of our life." "They could," says Secretary Ickes, without a visible smile at the curious comparison, "by means of tours and the radio be made to serve the country even more completely than does our national park system today."

Let us now consider how oddly Mr. Ickes reads Thomas Jefferson's phrase "pursuit of happiness." Seemingly, he reads it standing on his head. This posture is probably not noticeable in Washington where eccentricity meets so much competition, but between the covers of a book the sight still has the power to arouse a little wonder. Jefferson said "pursuit of." Mr. Ickes, being upside down, reads this as "pursuit by." He conjures up a picture of the New Democrat being energetically pursued right across our broad continent by orchestras and opera companies sent out by, perhaps, the Secretary of the Interior. Of course, his whole explanation of Jefferson's words is upside down. Jefferson was talking of equality of opportunity and the right to achieve and enjoy happiness, not the right to have it thrust upon one. These Utopians think of "pursuing" the citizen in the hope that they can overtake him and reward him for his lack of individual enterprise.

In "New Democracy," speaking of those who oppose his ideas, Ickes exclaims: "They must be stamped out regardless of their origin or status. . . ."

"Gangsters, racketeers, profiteers and chiselers," he says, meaning men who do not agree with him, "cannot be allowed to hamper or prevent the proper organization of the modern state. . . . Control over these desperadoes, of all types and classes, of both high and low degree, must lie in the government and that control must be firm and unrelenting in the interest of the people as a whole."

Mr. Ickes may on occasions, talk like one of the innocent, but always interesting, characters in "Alice in Wonderland," but there is another and a far more serious aspect of the man. It would take no great expert at contemporary research to find parallels to the above grim sentences in the speeches of Stalin, of Hitler, and of Mussolini, who also have often explained that, in Mr. Ickes words, "There is no dan-

ger in a strong government so long as it works un-
selfishly and disinterestedly for the whole people."
The contemporary dictators and those who would follow in their steps in the destruction of democracy
and the setting up of one-party, no-opposition, totalitarian states, agree perfectly.

"Our government is no longer a laissez-faire Government, exercising traditional and more or less impersonal powers." So, at least, Mr. Ickes informs us.

The French label here is oddly used. A laissez-
faire economy is an economy not interfered with by
the government. If a laissez-faire economy is one
not interfered with by the government, perhaps, by
the same rule, a laissez-faire government would be
a government not interfered with by economy? The
point here is that our Government, in Mr. Ickes'
opinion, has ceased to be traditional, impersonal.
Originally it was a government of principles, of impersonal laws. Now it is to be a government of men.
So were the ancient tyrannies; so is the modern totalitarian state. From the point of view of the political
faith of our fathers all these Minor Prophets are constitutional heretics. They are not restrained by any
respect for tradition or nationalism, but are zealous
to explore "New Frontiers" for an alien and foreign
scheme of life. All neo-tyrants chafe at the bit of restraint. They not only have an intellectual, a nerv-
ous, resentment against anything which tends to

bridle their actions, but also have a complex to be imperial in their dominance over others. When they fall from power, they declaim against their successors for continuing the very activities they themselves initiated, and blame these for persevering in the use of the authority which they themselves usurped. This is solely because these ousted tyrants are then the governed, not the governing. Their assumption is that Freedom is safe only in their hands.

It must not be overlooked that all these Minor Prophets occupy high official positions in the Administration and speak and write in their official capacities. The Administration, therefore, cannot disclaim official responsibility for their words so long as it permits them to hold themselves out in an official capacity, and we can properly and justly charge the Administration with officially sharing their views, even if we did not find such Administration endorsement in the Administration's policies and programs.

We shall now turn our attention to the Major Prophet himself!

CHAPTER VIII

THE MAJOR PROPHET

WE HAVE seen that the Minor Prophets of the New Deal are all thinking in the same political category; they all use the same nomenclature; they all have the same intellectual attitude toward our established institutions; and they all advance fundamentally the same solutions for our existing problems. They are not restrained by constitutional concepts, or by traditional loyalties, in their ardent desires and impetuous ambitions for the new order of society, which they so clearly and completely conceive and portray. They all display a religious zeal for the "Third Economy" under various appellations, in the apparent conviction that it is their divinely appointed mission to lead mankind to economic and social salvation through its saving grace. Their intentions are probably noble, but, by the patterns they are copying, their methods are demonstrated not to be what they claim them to be, but are rather means to inveigle the discontented and the unwary into the road that leads from Constitutional Democracy—Americanism—to an American adaptation of the New Despotisms.

Before his nomination for the presidency, Governor Roosevelt gave no indication of having any decided views of a politically or socially subversive nature, or of any desire on his part fundamentally to readjust our constitutional processes, to bring about any new order, or, in fact, in any way substantially to depart from the existing order. He seemed to look rather only to the perfecting of the existing order. His speeches while Governor of New York were all spoken in the mood of an orthodox constitutionalist seeking the correction of abuses, the reparation of wrongs, and social welfare for the people, through strictly constitutional means. He many times displayed a passionate devotion to States' rights as against Federal encroachments, and was always keen for the defense of individual liberty against governmental oppression. He boasted of being a true Jeffersonian democrat.

He was nominated and conducted his campaign on, and solemnly pledged himself to, the carrying out of all the provisions of the conservative and traditional platform adopted at the Democratic National Convention in 1932. This platform was declared to be "a covenant with the people," to state "the terms of the contract to which they (the people) are asked to subscribe." There is not a word in this platform which could, by even the most extravagant exaggeration, be said to foreshadow the "rounded whole" of his subsequent policies and actions. His campaign speeches did not seriously depart from this platform. Only once (and then merely casually, and, as some of his close advisers explained, unintentionally,) did he show an untraditional attitude toward, or disrespect for, the Supreme Court. As a matter of fact, even in his Inaugural Address, he said: "Our Constitution is so simple, so practical that it is possible always to meet extraordinary needs by changes in emphasis and arrangement without loss of essential form. That is why our constitutional system has proved itself the most superbly enduring political mechanism the world has ever seen."

It is clear, therefore, that when he took office in 1933, there was not, even in his own mind in any sense, a constitutional crisis before the country. As a matter of fact no one in a responsible position, or anybody officially identified with the incoming Administration, openly suggested any need or occasion for constitutional reform. The nation heard absolutely nothing which even remotely resembled the recent "professed objectives" of the members of his official family.

It is difficult for us to put our finger on the exact time, or to fix in our own minds the precise occasion, of the President's departure from the traditional way in our political thinking and of his entrance into the new road of thought and his taking the startlingly different direction thereon, which he is now so perversely pursuing. These changes seem to have developed surreptitiously, "unconsciously," as Wallace might say; or, perhaps, by "attrition," as Frankfurter, and Berle, would doubtlessly scientifically characterize the method of their development. Regardless, however, of when or how these melancholy changes took place it is all too painfully revealed by what we have read from the respective records of his official intimates, and which we have explained in the two immediately preceding Chapters of this book, that President Roosevelt's Administration is striving to make over the whole political and economic structure of our government, and of many of our social institutions.

When and how, therefore, President Roosevelt did develop "the distrust" for "the future of essential democracy," which he so eloquently disclaimed in his Inaugural Address, it is our disagreeable task, in this Chapter, to try to determine.

It cannot be successfully disputed that he assumed the presidency under most trying, almost desperate, conditions. The people gave him their practically unanimous acclaim. The responsibility he then took upon himself was extraordinary and stupendous, and was unprecedented. His courage gave the nation a renewed confidence. He knew and publicly stated that great sacrifices and drastic remedies were necessary, but he unhesitatingly proclaimed that our Constitution was able to meet "every stress."

The only hint of the possibility of any departure by him from our conventional theories and constitutional practices was that contained in the following paragraph of his Inaugural Address: "It is to be hoped that the normal balance of executive and legislative authority may be wholly adequate to meet the unprecedented task before us. But it may be that an unprecedented demand and need for undelayed action may call for temporary departure from the normal balance of public procedure." But he immediately made clear that he would seek only measures "within my constitutional authority."

It is significant to note that up to this time the Minor Prophets had not attained the prominence and power which they later did, at least not publicly, and that they had not as yet begun to preach their doctrines, or even their strange political, social, and economic views. Now looking back in retrospect, however, it is safe to assume that their unseen hands were even then at work, because we observe a striking similarity between their teachings and the legislative and executive program that was quickly developed and has since been assiduously pursued. This is surely more than a mere coincidence.

Soon we note that the President himself is conscious of the fact that the Administration policies are undertaking a new order of things and are effecting a permanent change in the existing order. He said "We have undertaken a new order of things . . . a permanent readjustment of many of our ways of thinking and therefore many of our social and economic arrangements." The implications of this are best explained by Wallace, who says: "The experimental method of democracy may be slow, but it has the advantage of being sure. When you change people's minds you change the course of a nation." The President, in his words quoted near the beginning of this paragraph, explicitly refers to "a new order of things" and to a "permanent readjustment of many of our ways of thinking," whereas at the commencement of his term, at most he only foresaw the possibility of "temporary departure." This reveals a progression in his thinking from temporary measures to meet unprecedented emergencies, to "permanent readjustment,"—and to the erection of a "new order."

Probably the complete plan or "blue-print" of this new order had not then fully matured in his mind, or, more likely, had not yet been entirely disclosed to him, but at least he realized that he "had undertaken a new order of things." His "ways of thinking," however, had changed considerably from the time of his inauguration. The record of the legislation which he initiated and imposed, and of his multitudinous activities under delegated powers, demonstrates the all-embracing scope of this new order. In earlier chapters we have described considerable of these activities so their repetition here is unnecessary. Our purpose now is to note the progress in President Roosevelt's thinking and action from that of a traditional constitutionalist to that of the builder of a new order, to be slowly constructed evidently on the plans furnished him by the Minor Prophets. There is certainly a close resemblance between his recent speeches and proposals and those of these Minor Prophets. The master and his disciples all seem tuned to the same rhythm, to be mentally travelling in the same direction. These Minor Prophets occupy key positions in the Administration and especially in those departments which lend themselves to economic and social experimentation. Their "blue-prints" always seem to fore-shadow, and to be the patterns for, all of the Administration's "must" legislation.

The President seems to have finally capitulated to their terms of an unconditional surrender: to a complete acceptance of the political ideals of these Prophets. He reveals a fundamentally different attitude toward our political institutions and constitutional processes in his address to Congress on the "State of the Union" on January 3, 1936 from the one he disclosed in his Inaugural Address on March 4, 1933. This message of January 3, 1936 is undoubtedly the most revealing, important, and startling address ever made by any Chief Magistrate of the United States. It must be most studiously analyzed and clearly understood by everyone who wishes to understand the real "State of the Union" today.

Even the occasion and circumstances of its delivery demand comment. The President is charged by the Constitution with the duty of informing Congress, from time to time, as to the "State of the Union." This duty has always been discharged solemnly and with a respectful deference to the dignity of the Legislative Branch of our Government. President Roosevelt desecrated this solemn occasion to utilize the rostrum of Congress as a broadcasting studio from which to make a political stump-speech to the nation on what might well be entitled the "State of the Presidential Campaign of 1936." He even selected the time which experience indicated would assure to him the largest possible radio audience. To all of this a benign, or perhaps a supine, Congress consented. The independence of the legislature from executive pressure and dominance has always been regarded as essential to the preservation of democratic government. Our Founding Fathers did their best to safeguard this, and no President until now has shown such disrespect for it.

Even in England, parliament preserves this doctrine as essential to the untrammeled legislative expression of the popular will. No King of England has entered the precincts of the House of Commons since the days of Charles I. He may enter only the House of Lords. According to the quaint procedure of the House of Commons, it would be possible to cause the withdrawal of even the Prince of Wales from the peer's gallery were a member ceremoniously to announce: "I spy strangers." This sentence is significant. The sovereign is a "stranger" to the popular branch of the government. This is no empty form. It has an historical importance and, by contrast with Mr. Roosevelt's recent conduct, is peculiarly instructive.

Now for his address!

He correctly diagnoses the "State of the Union" when he observes that: "within democratic nations the chief concern of the people is to prevent the continuance or the rise of autocratic institutions." That, indeed, is the theme and purpose of this entire book. We have not, however, here disposed of this "chief concern" by its mere observation, and by the use of the adjective "autocratic," but we have rather tried scientifically to compare our institutions, as those were bequeathed to us by the Founding Fathers, with the "professed objectives" and the activities of those at the present time composing our government, as well as with the objectives and accomplishments of the "New Despotisms" now affecting Europe, so as to judge for ourselves the right adjective to use correctly to describe these new "institutions." These precautions we find necessary because the New Dealers have a flippant way of misusing adjectives to serve their own particular purposes. They often mistake abuse for argument.

The President said: "You, the members of the legislative branch, and I, the Executive, contended for and established a new relationship between government and people."

What is this "new relationship" of which he so proudly boasts? The relationship between the United States Government and American citizens was established and defined by the written Constitution. This Constitution was the sovereign act of the sovereign people. It prescribes the only method by which it can be amended or changed. Therefore, the relationship which it established between government and people cannot be rightfully supplanted by any "new" relationship, except in the prescribed manner. This is a basic doctrine of Constitutional Democracy. But the President here says that a "new" relationship has been contended for and established by the concerted action of the legislative and executive branches. This seems a revolutionary method of amending the Constitution. The very intellectual conception that a relationship between government and people can be set up by means other than by the sovereign act of the people, and in the manner authorized by them, is diametrically opposed to our established doctrine of a government of laws, by solemn written compact with the sovereign people. It savors of the thought that the Executive with a dominated, or a willing, legislature is the source of our political institutions, and that they can rewrite our charter of government without popular consent. Moreover, if they have contended for and established this new relationship they have not reduced it to writing, as far as we know, and therefore they confess to supplanting impersonal, written law, with personal unwritten law. Perhaps, however, it is the President's thought that this new relationship was created by, and is found in, the recent legislative enactments. If this be so, then the foundations of that relationship have been repudiated by the Supreme Court as not built upon the Constitution.

If, however, it be contended that these "new" relationships were established by resort to constitutional processes, and that we have improperly construed the President's intended meaning, then we can only reply that the Supreme Court has not accepted his view. We do not intend to misinterpret these words of the President, but, frankly, if they mean anything to one who has the habit of constitutionally thinking, they must signify the meaning we see in them or they are just meaningless words. We must at any rate note in these words "a readjustment of many of our ways of thinking" toward our constitutional system.

The President further says "that in thirty-four months we have built up new instruments of public power" "on a broad base." Until "thirty-four months" ago we were content with the constitutional instruments of public power—they were the only instruments of public power the people ever built up—constructed on the fundamental and sole base of our Constitution. "Instruments of public power" have been variously named by his circle of political experimenters, as we have seen, as "social discipline," "public control," "democratic discipline," and "planned economy"; and Dr. Tugwell has also spoken of "creating institutions," and of the "public authority to achieve the necessary control." We here observe that the President himself is also thinking in the same terms of extending the "sphere" of governmental activity by new instruments, by new controls. We finally get the "rounded whole" of all their independent thinking canalized in one approach to the "New Frontiers." "Autocrats in smaller things, they seek autocracy in bigger things." That is the progression. Their united efforts seem to be directed toward expanding the "frontiers" of our political and constitutional institutions into an instrumentality to set up the "New Order" and to do so by manipulating constitutional processes into "new instruments of public power."

The Supreme Court, in speaking of the A.A.A., "the Constitution of an economic government," which so perfectly embodied the philosophy of all these Minor Prophets, and which the Major Prophet found so satisfactory, said:

"Until recently no suggestion of the existence of any such power in the Federal Government has been advanced. The expressions of the framers of the Constitution, the decisions of this court interpreting that instrument, and the writings of great commentators will be searched in vain for any suggestion that there exists in the clause under discussion [the taxation clause], or elsewhere in the Constitution, the authority whereby every provision and every fair implication from that instrument may be subverted, the independence of the individual States obliterated, and the United States converted into a central government exercising uncontrolled police power in every State of the Union, superseding all local control or regulation of the affairs or concerns of the State."

We can imagine no language which could more clearly reveal the totalitarian tendencies of this legislative expression of the "professed objectives" of the New Dealers, and more severely condemn them as destructive of the institutions of Americanism.

It is interesting to observe that the Supreme Court notes that "until recently no suggestion of any such power in the Federal Government has been advanced" which seems to confirm the President's statement that it is entirely within the last "thirty-four months," that is only since his accession to power, and while he and his Administration were "writing a new chapter in the history of popular government," that even a "suggestion" of these "new instruments of public power" were ever advanced. This practically fixes the time of the introduction of these totalitarian concepts into the scheme of our Government.

Now, how can we reconcile this "new chapter in the history of popular government" with the preceding chapters written by the Founding Fathers, in the Declaration of Independence and in the Constitution of the United States? It seems to us, when we compare the doctrine contended for by the President and his advisers with that of the previous chapters, that they have not written merely a new chapter, but rather an entirely new and different book. Where do we find in this "new chapter" reverence for the sacred rights of man which are his by divine endowment and are beyond interference by the State? Where do we find respect for the distribution of powers into different and independent political units? What has happened to local self-government in the States? What has become of the organic structure of our constitutional machinery, which, as we have seen, was carefully set up to prevent the concentrating of power? Where do we observe any thought that the Constitution is a solemn compact between the people and the Government, which the Government must obey if the people's "consent" is to be respected? Where are the basic institutions upon which our Government and our traditions have been erected? The Supreme Court has thus far sought in vain for them therein.

On the other hand, this "new chapter" fits perfectly into all the "bibles" of the Prophets of the New Deal —Wallace's "New Frontiers," Ezekiel's "$2,500 a Year," and Ickes' "The New Democracy," and into the expositions of "Social Discipline" by Richberg and of the "Third Economy" of Tugwell. These are all commentaries on the same political philosophy. All these authors of the "new chapter in the history of popular government" belong to the same school of political thought. Their chapter in political history might well be entitled "Democratic Despotism," or the "American Totalitarian State."

"But," our President tells us, "in the hands of political puppets of any economic autocracy such power would provide shackles for the liberties of the people." Let us read this statement in the light of the objectives of the Minor Prophets and from the record of the legislative enactments, and of the executive activities, of the past "thirty-four months," and see if its true meaning does not unfold itself!

Certainly, the "Third Economy," the "New Frontiers," the "New Democracy," "Social Discipline," the "New Order," most comprehensively "blue-print" a perfect and complete "economic autocracy." Has any economic, social, or human, activity been left out of their "spheres" of governmental authority and control? The legislative record also presents a "fairly rounded whole"—manufacture, mining, agriculture, banking, finance, credit, transportation, communications, public utilities, housing, industrial relations, social security, etc.—practically all economic enterprises and activities. Does not that give a fairly detailed manifestation of "economic autocracy"? Surely, no comparable control over our economic and social life was ever contended for by any other group or individual. Other economic autocrats, if there be any, are mere little fish alongside of this Leviathan. If such a concentration of economic power provides "shackles for the liberties of the people," as it most certainly does, then those possessed of this power can justify themselves only on the theory that they alone can be trusted with such power.

We recall the admonition of our ancestors that the concentration of power in any one political unit, no matter how democratic it may be, is despotism. Moreover, the people have never expressed any desire for a dictator even though he be wise and good. Our President, however, seems to revert to the spirit of our ancestors when he wisely observes: "Give them their way and they will take the course of every autocracy of the past—power for themselves, enslavement for the public." He might also have added the autocracies of the present to his denunciation of those of the past. Europe demonstrates that this political principle is as true today as it has been throughout the whole course of history.

Another statement in this speech of President Roosevelt further confirms a line of thinking foreign to our political concepts. "We have returned the control of the Federal Government to the city of Washington." Heretofore, the control of the Federal Government resided in the forty-eight sovereign States and the people. Part of the machinery and some of its operations have always been conveniently located in Washington. Many of the elected officials, and some of the appointed agents, of the Federal Government also carry on their assigned functions there. But *control* is a different thing. We have tried to make it clear that one of the fundamental concepts of our constitutional philosophy is to prohibit the concentration of power—the deposit of control—in any one political unit, as President Washington said in his Farewell Address, "by dividing and distributing it into different depositories." We should again be reminded that the Supreme Court has sounded the warning that the deposit of control in any political unit, no matter how democratic, is despotism. Apparently President Roosevelt does not accept this fundamental concept of our constitutional system, or he is here only phrase-making for political effect without really intending to say what his words actually signify and imply.

This speech of the President is of epoch-making importance. If it were merely an emotional out-burst on the political stump, and it stood alone and apart from the "professed objectives" of his key men, and did not so clearly explain the constitutional philosophy behind so much of his Administrative activities and the legislation inspired and demanded by him, then we would be unjustified in giving it such significance. But, unfortunately, that is not the case. This speech fits perfectly into the philosophy and activities of himself and of the active leaders in his Administration. It completes our understanding of the constitutional "psychology" and philosophy of the "new chapter in the history of popular government."

President Roosevelt has evidently progressed far since his inauguration. Possibly the master has been intellectually corrupted by his disciples. General Hugh Johnson, who should know the inner workings and secret confidences of the chosen few, seems to have this opinion, because he said on November 8th,

1935: "He (the President) is being pulled and hauled into impractical paths by visionary associates." At any rate, it is only too evident that they all now pursue exactly the same line of thought and action.

In his Inaugural Address the President said, "The money-changers have fled from their high seats in the temple of our civilization. We may now restore that temple to the ancient truths."

If this be true, the high seats seem now to be occupied by priests of some strange creed, as they do not appear to be preaching the "ancient truths" of our Constitution, but rather to be practicing the rites of some foreign cult, which greatly resembles totalitarianism. With misgiving hearts we observe these priests of strange gods in the temple of our American civilization, and we are very fearful that in purging the temple of its money-changers the Prophets of the New Deal may have admitted these false priests, and that, like Sampson of old, they may topple the whole temple and bring it down in ruins, not only on their own devoted heads, and on the political Philistines, but also upon the person and the property of the great mass of our citizens.

President Roosevelt in his book "Looking Forward" confesses to being conscious that great change in our economic life has become imminent. He says: "I believe that we are at the threshold of a fundamental change in our economic thought." He might truthfully have added that we have already crossed the threshold of the "New Frontiers" and are well "On Our Way." A clever technique has been used to carry us "On Our Way," and as this technique is dedicated to effecting "fundamental change," it can be correctly described as "The Technique of 'The Revolution.'"

CHAPTER IX

THE TECHNIQUE OF "THE REVOLUTION"

WE HAVE seen that our traditional democratic ideas have been violently distorted, and our constitutional concepts manhandled, by a coterie of visionaries, appointed to non-elective key positions, and that the President himself has progressed under their tutelage to a practical acceptance of their "professed objectives." We have seen that the New Deal was not included in the Democratic platform of 1932. It was rather evolved from the motives and ideals of those who sprang out of the unknown after the election. We are now confronted with a universal belief in the philosophy of the "New Order" by all those composing the directive force of the New Deal. There is every reason, therefore, why the alert and the inquiring should endeavor to determine the direction that the New Deal is giving to our political thinking, and to understand the professed ideals of individual freedom, and of the political institutions of the new social and political order, which its votaries visualize and strive to achieve. Surely, it has been "blue-printed" sufficiently clearly, and with enough detail, to give us an acquaintance with it adequate to predicate a reasoned opinion thereon as to whether or not it is the system of society which we would prefer to our present system. Beyond any question of doubt, we are, at least, convinced that it is basically different from our American system of constitutional democracy and is absolutely incompatible therewith. It has a striking resemblance in its fundamental thoughts with certain European philosophies which we have called "The New Despotisms."

We should, therefore, observe, record, and analyze the technique being employed to attain these aims and objects, in order to ascertain what efforts have been made toward their realization, and to learn the exact nature of these endeavors.

To gain power by a cunning misuse of democratic methods is the most generally adopted technique of all astute politicians, who are planning to destroy, for their own self-seeking purposes, cherished governmental theories and institutions, and history proves it to be more efficacious, and certainly less perilous, than violence. Revolution is the exceptional, and the last-recourse, method. But once having democratically assumed power, the beginnings of an early transition to despotism become noticeable. The party names, platforms, and principles, which were utilized as a means to gain power are remolded to fit the real motives and ideals of the incipient usurpers.

The New Dealers followed this historic pattern. They rode into power on the political machine of the Democratic Party. They paraded, and still parade, as Democrats though their "professed objectives," as we have observed them, are far removed from anything that traditional Democrats ever professed. General Johnson said on January 7, 1936: "I gravely protested an infiltration of inexperienced young socialists in practical control of an Administration not elected as socialist. . . . That is almost political fraud." Certainly, he was in "on the know" during the campaign and in the first years of the Administration.

Henry Wallace most clearly explains the situation:

"So enlisted, men may rightfully feel they are serving a function as high as that of any minister of the Gospel. They will not be Socialists, Communists or Fascists, but plain men trying to gain *by democratic methods the professed objectives of the Communists, Socialists and Fascists; . . .*" (Italics Ours.)

That accurately describes the technique which they have adopted. They "will not be Socialists, Communists or Fascists" by openly and officially aligning themselves with those parties, or identifying themselves with their organized activities, "even though they are trying to gain the professed objectives of the Communists, Socialists and Fascists," so long as they are hopefully seeking to attain these "professed objectives" "by democratic methods."

They purpose deceitfully to use party labels and machinery, to manipulate democratic processes, to maneuver democratic forces, and finally, as we will soon see, to convert, improperly, constitutional machinery to the furtherance of their designs.

Let us, therefore, briefly pursue the record of the use of this technique!

Wallace says: "The experimental method of democracy may be slow, but it has the advantage of being sure. When you change people's minds you change the course of a nation." To divert the nation's course, we are naively told, we must first "change people's minds." We must free them from their intellectual bondage to outworn and obsolete ideals. We must demonstrate that their traditional institutions, their constitutional processes and limiations, are outmoded and inadequate under new conditions, arrest progress, and prevent man from achieving his new destiny, from realizing his new promise. We must, therefore, give a new direction to political thought.

The "scientific" approach, however, requires that

we must not directly and openly attack the efficacy of the existing systems, as this might shock the people's susceptibilities and thereby make them hesitant to change, but we should rather step by step prepare the people's minds for a gradual and unconscious acceptance of the new ideas. We have already seen the subtle maneuvers made to impregnate our political thinking with new economic and social concepts, by demonstrating that our economic and social advances demand the expansion of political agencies into economic controls, by guiding our reason and imagination through our present constitutional confines across "New Frontiers" into "social discipline," "planned economy," and the "Third Economy." But teaching must be pursued by action!

The people having been thus made impressionable and receptive to these new ideas by the distortion of democratic ideas, the next step is to manipulate democratic processes in such a manner as to convert these new ideas into accomplished fact. "We must go forward with the Constitution"; that is, as long as the Constitution can be molded to their purpose.

As "human beings respond far more readily to psychological than to logical arguments," again to use Mr. Wallace's revealing words, the appeal is directed to man's emotions. Advantage is taken of human suffering and distress. A new hope is offered. Permanent security is promised. The geography of a new land of promise is pictured in beguiling words. Our humanitarian instincts are aroused. Psychological arguments are exhausted. Events are dramatized to play on human emotions. The new "leaders" portray themselves as the way, the truth, and the life.

A crusade to purge the body politic of those persons and forces that are blamed, with or without reason, for everything that delays the consummation of the new order, is piously and fervently launched. A thirst for revenge is stimulated. All these aroused emotions are concentrated and directed against their predecessors in power and against those who still believe in the faith of their fathers. Star Chamber investigations are conducted. Invective and vituperation, growing in their ferocity by their own impetus, become customary political jargon. Class animosities are stirred up. "The Bourbons are responsible for everything" is an old slogan. "We must declare and win our independence from the Tories," has a familiar sound. Political adventurers usually use the stereotyped formula of recruiting an army of the discontented and of then regimenting them for their self-advancement.

All of these are the "psychological arguments" always employed. They are part of the historic and universal technique.

Therefore, these advocates of the "new order" first sought a constitutional refuge in attempting to utilize so-called emergency powers to meet emergency conditions. This was an emotionally appealing recourse. It aroused a humanitarian and patriotic sympathy in us all. Obviously, sacrifices must be made to meet emergencies, the individual must subordinate his selfish interest to the general salvation. No one will deny that individual rights cannot be arbitrarily exercised without due regard to the promotion of the paramount general welfare. But, unless the accommodation of individual rights to the public welfare, even in emergencies, is made through constitutional processes, the principle that the sovereign can abrogate or suspend such rights is admitted. Such a doctrine is clearly alien and distasteful to *our* constitutional philosophy, and tends in the direction of the omnipotent or totalitarian State possessed of unlimited power.

But let us confront this "psychological" appeal with "logical arguments," which Wallace recognizes as not being so convenient for his purposes. Our Founding Fathers well understand the oppressive potentialities latent in emergency powers, and that such powers lead to "anarchy or despotism." In spite of the Civil War emergency which gave rise to the statute providing for military trials in espionage cases, Justice Davis, speaking for the Supreme Court, said:

"Time has proven the discernment of our ancestors; for even these provisions, expressed in such plain English words that it would seem the ingenuity of man could not evade them, are *now*, after the lapse of more than seventy years, sought to be avoided. Those great and good men foresaw that troublous times would arise, when rulers and people would become restive under restraint, and seek by sharp and decisive measures to accomplish ends deemed just and proper; and that the principles of constitutional liberty would be in peril, unless established by irrepealable law. The history of the world had taught them that what was done in the past might be attempted in the future. The Constitution of the United States is a law for rulers and people, equally in war and in peace, and covers with the shield of its protection all classes of men, at all times, and under all circumstances. No doctrine, involving more pernicious consequences, was ever invented by the wit of man than that any of its provisions can be suspended during any of the great exigencies of government. *Such a doctrine leads directly to anarchy or despotism, but the theory of necessity on which it is based is false;* for the government, within the Constitution, has all the powers granted to it, which are necessary to preserve its existence; as has been happily proved by the result of the great effort to throw off its just authority." (Italics Ours.)

Although the Supreme Court has given several examples of its recognition of the exigencies of emergencies, it has repeatedly affirmed the doctrine that emergencies do not create powers not expressly given, but only furnish the occasion for the use of granted powers.

The Supreme Court has clearly enunciated this principle in the *Schechter* case:

"We are told that the provision of the statute authorizing the adoption of codes must be viewed in the light of the grave national crisis with which Congress was confronted. Undoubtedly, the conditions to which power is addressed are always to be considered when the exercise of power is challenged. Extraordinary conditions may call for extraordinary remedies. But the argument necessarily stops short of an attempt to justify action which lies outside the sphere of constitutional authority. Extraordinary conditions do not create or enlarge constitutional power."

It is mere assumption, presumption if you please, to assert that recent emergencies could not be met by means other than those chosen, and by methods which were *within* the Constitution. And also it is open to serious question if any emergency can be so great as to justify the permanent abandonment of our entire political philosophy or system of government. At any rate, there is every reason for us to refuse to forsake our institutions until it has been most clearly demonstrated that there is no other recourse.

History is replete with illustrations of temporary emergencies being utilized as a means to gain permanent power, and in fact, of instances, where emergencies were "created" as pretexts for the seizure of power. "Emergencies demand emergency action and emergency action requires emergency power" is not a novel formula in the technique of revolution. Emergency legislation or action must also be carefully studied to make certain that it is in fact and is really intended only to meet emergency conditions. Too often emergency action is transformed into permanent policy. For instance, the President had announced the A.A.A. as a permanent agricultural policy before it was declared unconstitutional. We have already seen how, abroad, dictators rode to absolute power during emergencies which they themselves partially precipitated and encouraged, or at least converted to their uses.

Emergency powers thus proving inadequate for their purposes, recourse was next had by the Prophets of the New Deal to the Commerce Clause in the Constitution as a possible vehicle for extending Federal controls and discipline. They sought to extend the heretofore well defined limitations of interstate commerce so as to include not only instrumentalities of interstate commerce but all activities of production—such as manufacturing, mining and crop-growing—on the theory that such production burdened or affected the free current or flow of interstate commerce, and that wage distributions (to use one illustration) "provide the necessary stimulus in starting the cumulative forces making for expanding commercial activity." Here the effort is simply to expand the "sphere" of governmental control under the claim that present economic conditions have themselves brought these economic activities within the constitutional "sphere." This effort perfectly illustrates the practical operations of Dr. Tugwell's technique for erecting the "Third Economy" by judicial interpretation.

It is an effort to erect upon a single enumerated power an inverted pyramid of such proportions as to be all-inclusive and to threaten to expand the limited Federal Government into a general and absolute sovereignty. If the possible consequences were not so tragic, it would be intellectually entertaining to observe the extension of such metaphysical conceptions as that by which the "effect of interstate obstructions on the so-called flow or current of interstate commerce," can become a subterfuge for the creation of Federal control over practically all local matters. The Commerce Clause cannot be used as a Juggernaut mercilessly to ride over and crush all State and individual rights. The Supreme Court has time and again defined its restricted application.

The Supreme Court has recently said:

"If the commerce clause were construed to reach all enterprises and transactions which could be said to have an indirect effect upon interstate commerce, the Federal authority would embrace practically all the activities of the people and the authority of the State over its domestic concerns would exist only by sufferance of the Federal government. Indeed, on such a theory, even the development of the State's commercial facilities would be subject to Federal control. . . ."

Moreover, activities, which are essentially and inherently local in character, cannot be brought within the "sphere" of Federal power by a congressional declaration that they "directly affect" interstate commerce. Realities control; not the wishful reasoning, or the dogmatic declarations, of the interpretative expansionists.

Again, finding this second constitutional recourse also inadequate, they seize upon another constitutional power of the Federal Government—the taxing power—hopeful that it may prove to be the means of furthering them toward their goal. Taxation has been, and is, increasingly being used not only as a means to raise revenues for purposes and objects within the scope of the enumerated functions of the Federal Government, but also as a punitive weapon, as an instrument of economic control, and as a means to set up industrial standards. "Taxation," as an instrument, has been already utilized to regulate production, sale, and distribution of agricultural, mining and industrial products, and their related activities; to subsidize one class at the expense of another; and is being proposed as a means to prevent the concentration of wealth and of economic power, and as a remedy against the "bigness" of business.

Government funds are being appropriated to a multitude of purposes not restricted to objects germane to its delegated powers, on the principle that the Federal Government has unlimited power to appropriate money for the promotion of the "general welfare," and also because emergency conditions justify abnormal expenditures, even for private enterprises, State and local developments, and relief, which are not in themselves national in character. Government is competing with private business and is establishing "yard-sticks" with which to measure and coerce private business. The "spheres" of Federal activity are being extended through the benefit of appropriations, and by coercive penalties inflicted upon the recalcitrants. Power is being concentrated in the Executive arm of the Federal Government through its granting of financial favors.

Now, of course, taxation was originally conceived as the means of raising money for the support of the Government: revenue for the carrying on of Governmental activities as such activities were then understood, not for the support of all industrial, agricultural and other economic activities, and social welfare enterprises. With these the Government was certainly supposed to have no concern. Thus to expand the Federal Government from a political instrumentality into a paternal agency for social service, and into a means of economic promotion for each individual citizen, is surely a far departure from the early limited conception of our Federal Government.

Now, this is not an appropriate occasion to debate the wisdom or propriety of any of these social and economic concerns, but only to emphasize the method used to bring them within the "spheres" of the "Constitution of an economic government."

Purchasing submission to "social discipline" and acceptance of the "Third Economy," by rewarding, with tax rebates amounting to as much as ninety per cent of the tax assessment, those who "voluntarily" consent, by agreement, to the government's exactions, is what we might call constitutional immorality. Liberty has its price but it should not be bought with governmental bribery. This is a corrupting doctrine.

Furthermore, the tax is so computed and assessed that anyone not obtaining the rebate, is left at such a competitive disadvantage with those who do accept that he cannot continue in his business profitably, if, indeed, at all. To estop a citizen from asserting his constitutional rights by purchasing his surrender is a stultifying innovation shocking to any man proud of his birthright.

Many of these abusive uses of the taxing power have already been condemned and forbidden, but there are yet other fields to be explored in its use under the Supreme Court's interpretation of "general welfare" in the taxing clause. We already note the avidity with which the *obiter dicta* in the *Hoosac Mills Case* is being turned to by these technicians.

But they have still other arrows in their quivers! They still have other "instruments of public power"! They grasp at the power of Congress to regulate the use of the mails. They attempt to expand this power, intended only to assure the proper, honest, and efficient use of the mails, into an instrument of absolute control, under which the mail is open only to those, and for only such purposes, as the government may choose. If this power may be employed to deny access to the mails in the absolute discretion of Congress, then this device can be utilized to bring all business under control, and even to impose a censorship.

The Securities Act, the Securities and Exchange Act, and the Public Utility Holding Company Act, already have converted this power to new objectives. Truly, it is all a question of degree, but we must be cautious in yielding the principle involved, for once the principle is established, its extension becomes more easy and more dangerous.

Federal jurisdiction over navigable streams has been elaborated into the Federal Government's engaging in the generation, transmission, and sale of electrical energy, and in the manufacture and retail sale of electric appliances in competition with private business and to create "yard-sticks" with which to establish rate structures. Here again it is a question of degree. It is a question of how far the original "sphere" of a granted power may be rightfully enlarged from its original intent to extend it into new fields, which have arisen from economic development and invention.

Without judicial restraint upon its expansion, the Federal power might be inflated until it expanded far beyond the limits essential to safeguard our basic constitutional institutions.

We are carried still further along by these expansionist interpretations. Mr. Richberg insinuated, and others claim, that the general welfare clause in the Preamble of the Constitution and in Section 8 of Article I, confers unlimited and plenary power on

Congress to legislate in the interest of the general welfare. This legalistic sophistry is not even novel or original. The courts have long since, and repeatedly, held that "the Preamble never can be resorted to, to enlarge the powers confided in the general government or any of its departments. It cannot confer any power *per se*." And the phrase "general welfare" in Section 8 of Article I has been held to be purely a limitation upon the taxing power by defining the purpose for which taxes can be levied. The argument, therefore, of Mr. Richberg and those who agree with him, can only be predicated on the premise, (1), that the Preamble is the entire Constitution and that everything which follows it must be totally disregarded as an irrelevant postscript, or, (2), that the words "general welfare" in Section 8 of Article I confer a general power instead of being a limitation of the taxing power. If the latter be the correct interpretation, how can you explain away the enumeration of specific powers, because if the phrase "general welfare" can be construed to grant any powers, then that phrase is sufficiently broad unquestionably to comprehend all sovereign powers, and there would be, therefore, no need to enumerate or specify any particular powers.

Mr. Richberg and others seem to like to juggle these soap bubbles and to entertain, if not, indeed, to confuse, us with a discussion as to whether the original text of Article I, Section 8, of the Constitution was not surreptitiously, or accidentally, altered by changing the punctuation in such a way as completely to change the meaning of this Section. These arguments are all purely hypothetical but they betray the mentality of an iconoclast, and reveal a disrepectful attitude toward our Constitution, which would be amusing, if it was not so dangerous under present conditions.

What constitutes a legitimate use of taxes in the "general welfare" remains to be definitely established by judicial interpretation, it only being our present intention here to give another illustration of how audaciously some of these Minor Prophets attempt to distort our Constitution and to confuse our thinking. It will be interesting to see what new constituional magic they will try when their present bag of tricks is exhausted.

Thus far they have met with an unsurmountable obstacle in the process of this technique—the Judiciary. Fearing that this is a barrier they cannot jump, they now propose either to remove it as a barrier, or so to impair it, that it will not block their progress. They make a variety of proposals to deprive the Supreme Court of its power to declare legislation and executive acts unconstitutional. Chief among these are: to require a unanimous decision, or a majority opinion of seven, to void such acts;

to increase the number of the Justices composing the Supreme Court and to pack it with "liberals"; and to restrict the judicial power of injunction in all cases against the Government. All of these proposals have the same objectives—to remove restraint on their power to interpret and apply the Constitution in furtherance of their desires. They are resentful, at times bitter, against a supreme law to which their wills must bend and which they must obey. They want a government of men—themselves —not of laws.

The Administration in its political caution thus far withholds its official support to all of these measures, but it is significant that it does not repudiate or disavow even those in the official family who openly encourage such views. Perhaps astute observers have reported that as yet there has not been a sufficient change in the people's minds to justify such a political risk. At any rate its satellites continue their campaign of education.

In addition to these efforts to remove the obstacles of the Constitution, they next obviously find themselves embarrassed by the restraint of impersonal law: law which is not entirely subject to their will. We find latent in their conception of law—and some have been publicly preaching this view—that law emanates solely from the will of the majority of the people, and can, therefore, be modified at any time to meet majority wishes. This doctrine is absolutely totalitarian, and is contrary to our basic conceptions of the source of law. We have seen that our political system is predicated on the doctrine that there are some immutable laws of nature and certain other divinely sanctioned rights, which the Constitution and our tradition recognized as being above and beyond the power of the majority, or of any other group of individuals or officials of the Government. There are, also, other rights, which because of man's historic experience, that are specifically protected by the Constitution, and which can only be modified under the prescribed method set forth in the Constitution; and, consequently the majority-will is not free to modify them as it pleases, but only in the circumscribed manner prescribed by the Constitution. That is why our system has been characterized as a government *of laws, not of men*. That is the distinction between impersonal law and personal law. Americanism is the system of government by impersonal law: totalitarianism is the system of government by personal law.

To hold that *all* law emanates from popular will implies that the decision of the majority is by its nature impartial and just toward all and that no restrictions to protect minorities and individuals are necessary. Historical experience shows that that is contrary to the fact. Our Constitution, and especially our Bill of Rights, were designed from this experience and were intended to prevent violation, by majorities or by powerful governmental groups, of the basic rights recognized as beyond governmental interference. If this was not the fact, man would exist and live at the will of every transient majority, and his natural and inalienable rights would exist in name only. All human institutions and individual rights would be the creature of mass emotionalism, and would have no protection against the foibles of each fleeting moment.

Obviously, there are, on the other hand, many respects in which majority-will does and should control. Our Constitution affords the fullest expression of majority-will in all fields *except* only those in which certain rights are expressly reserved. Of course, no such exceptions exist in a pure democracy, but, as we have shown, that is not the political system which we have. In some countries, tradition and national culture have acted as a restraining influence on majority action, but, as we have pointed out, our Constitution is our tradition, and we would find ourselves in a different situation, if the Constitution were removed. Nothing is more fundamental than this doctrine to the preservation of our institutions—in fact, it is the bulwark of our constitutional freedom—and, therefore, the advocacy of views destructive of it is easy to understand but alarming to contemplate. It is, however, an essential part of the technique employed.

The President himself urged Congress to pass a bill notwithstanding "doubts as to constitutionality, however reasonable."   Congress itself seems perfectly willing to enact laws without any great legal scrutiny and to pass them on to the courts for final decision as to their constitutionality. We would hesitate to accuse the Administration with deliberately planning to accumulate laws of questionable validity, or of known invalidity, and with passing the responsibility to the courts of deciding this point, so that a record could be made that it is the courts which are thwarting the popular will, but for the fact that one who has enjoyed high Presidential favor and has been circumstanced in his official contacts so as to be able to speak knowingly, said in respect of the necessity of meeting "issues faster":

"One group, as you know, headed by my friend Professor Frankfurter of Harvard is rather anxious that this should be done by getting the Supreme Court gradually to modify its views. I think the famous phrase is 'judicial attrition.'   In practice this means serving up case after case in the hope that the court will modify its more dogmatic statements, its very broad dicta about interstate commerce. Another group prefers to do the job directly by debating the question of whether we should or should not amend the Constitution."

These are words of Prof. A. A. Berle, Jr. (July, 1935).

Dr. Tugwell assumes a different, but yet a defiant, attitude in describing his impatience with judicial restraint interposed against the acceptance of his views; for he said, in his University of New Mexico speech apropos of the *Schechter* decision, that the *Schechter* decision gave rise to a constitutional crisis "quite as great as one of war," and that the industrial revolution moved too fast "for the accommodation of judicial theory." The words "revolution," and more especially "judicial theory," as applied to a unanimous decision of the Supreme Court, cannot be idly dismissed without serious apprehension. This is a perfect expression of his contempt for law which blocks his progress. "Judicial theory," by which he oddly means law, must be amenable to his will, it must be "accommodated" to his "revolution." How, by "judicial attrition" or nullification, he does not say.

There is evidently a concerted and deliberate plan to destroy public confidence in the courts, so as to lay a foundation for removing them as barriers to meeting "issues faster," and for "the accommodation of judicial theory"; that is to say, to hasten to replace

Americanism by the "Third Economy" and to "adapt" our law to suit its demands. One can conceive of a no more subtle and malicious subterfuge to undermine the very corner-stones of our institutions.

Too long, far too long, it is to be feared, the citizenry of this country and also the Supreme Court of the United States have been patient with the strategy and the tactics of the Prophets of the New Deal. In this connection it is well for us to meditate deeply on the wisdom of what Chief Justice Hughes writes in his book: "The Supreme Court of the United States." Citing with approval Judge Bradley in the case of *Boyd vs. United States* (1886), he tells us how best to resist the destruction of our institutions by interpretive expansionists, and by "judicial attrition." He says:

"It was in this opinion that Justice Bradley sounded his eloquent warning against permitting invasions of constitutional rights because they were of a relatively mild and but slightly offensive character; 'illegitimate and unconstitutional practices get their first footing in that way, namely: by silent approaches and slight deviations from legal modes of procedure. This can only be obviated by adhering to the rule that constitutional provisions for the security of persons and property should be liberally construed. A close and literal construction deprives them of half of their efficacy and leads to gradual depreciation of the right, as if it consisted more in sound than in substance. It is the duty of the courts to be watchful for the constitutional rights of the citizen, and against any stealthy encroachments thereon. Their motto should be obsta principiis.' "

This warning, to "oppose encroachments at the start" is more needed today than ever in our history; it is the technique with which to oppose their technique.

The technique, herein briefly recorded, has, in many of its most important manifestations, been examined by the Supreme Court, and its unrevealed and obscure implications, not only fully explained, but severely condemned. The judiciary has again proved itself to be the bulwark of defense against the subtle and skilful manipulation of democratic processes to achieve unsanctioned theories. We will find great instruction in even briefly reviewing these "Ghosts that Walked in the Night," these shadows of despotism which were momentarily cast over our institutions of liberty.

CHAPTER X

GHOSTS THAT WALKED IN THE NIGHT

THE record of the actual efforts already made to establish the "New Order," and to apply the theories of the New Despotisms, through the technique of manipulating our constitutional processes, is voluminous. Great progress "On Our Way," "Forward with the Constitution," is to be noted. Theories were developed into realities. The "blue-prints" were reduced to legislation, and the erection of the New Order, "on a broad base," by the "new instruments of public power," was started. Many actual steps in the evolutionary process of changing "the course of the nation" have already been taken. In this Chapter we purpose to consider only those attempts which have failed; those "blue-prints" which were rejected by the Supreme Court as wholly foreign to our constitutional concepts. The record conclusively demonstrates that there has been an actual attempt to revamp the foundations and to remodel the structure of our Government in exact accord with the "professed objectives" of these official theorists.

Clearly to understand the obscure implications

and the real consequences of these legislative efforts
and the ultimate goal of their direction, we should
measure them, first, with the yard-stick of the constitutional principles of Americanism, and second,
with the yard-stick of the ideas and ideals of their
sponsors and defenders. The Supreme Court could
not "square" the legislative pillars of the New Deal
with the Constitution; could not fit them into the
framework of our institutions; and, therefore, rejected them as alien to our constitutional system.
The discussion of these legislative efforts, is, however,
not merely academic, because these not only depict
the technique of "The Revolution" in operation,
but, more especially, because they reveal that some
of the spoken words of the Prophets came to life.
They all cast a decipherable shadow of totalitarianism over our institutions. When these ghosts of the
New Despotisms were brought into the daylight of
popular view by the discerning eyes of the Supreme
Court, they were recognized for what they really
were, and were banished with popular acclaim to the
graveyard of tyranny from whence they came. While
they stalked amongst us, we were forcibly impressed
with the fact that they foreshadowed the "professed
objectives" of the new Prophets of the totalitarian
State.

Now for a seance with a few of these ghosts!

The National Industrial Recovery Act was condemned by the Supreme Court in the *Schechter* and in the *Panama Refining Company* cases, because that Act asserted a jurisdiction, and attempted to set up a form of control over industry, which was beyond the power of the Federal Government to establish. The Supreme Court emphatically said, in the *Schechter* case, that that Act violated both the principle of dual sovereignty—of the States and of the Federal Government—and the principle of the separation of powers within the Federal Government. It not only attempted an unconstitutional concentration of power in the Federal Government, but it also endeavored to lodge that concentrated power in the Executive. The Supreme Court especially condemned the attempt of Congress to delegate its lawmaking functions to the President. The Court significantly observed in the *Panama Refining Company* Case: "The question is not of the intrinsic importance of the particular statute before us, but of the constitutional processes of legislation which are an essential part of our system of government." "Essential," indeed; as we have seen, because those constitutional processes were created and distributed to prevent the concentration of power in any one political unit, lest this concentration be used, as is customarily done, to bring about tyranny.

The Supreme Court noted not merely a voluntary delegation by Congress of its law-making functions to the President, but rather a supine abdication of these powers in his favor, stimulated, probably, by Presidential cajoling, and, perhaps, by a little "political," or persuasive, pressure. The words of the Supreme Court in this connection are:

"The Congress is not permitted to abdicate or to transfer to others the essential legislative functions with which it is thus vested. . . . Congress cannot delegate legislative power to the President to exercise an unfettered discretion to make whatever laws he thinks may be needed or advisable for the rehabilitation and expansion of trade or industry."

Again, in the *Humphrey* Case, the Supreme Court said:

"The fundamental necessity of maintaining each of the three general departments of government entirely free from the *control* or *coercion*, direct or indirect, of either of the others, has often been stressed and is hardly open to serious question. So much is implied in the very fact of the separation of the powers." (Italics Ours.)

The argument that expeditious and effective action in the public good could be obtained in emergency conditions only through vesting the President with discretionary power to act without the delay usually incidental to congressional action, and that that was the sole motive of this exceptional delegation of legislative power to him, was rather decisively disposed of by the Supreme Court in the *Panama Refining Company* Case:

"The question whether the delegation of legislative power is permitted by the Constitution is not answered by the argument that it should be assumed that the President has acted, or will act, for what he believes to be the public good. The point is not one of motives but of constitutional authority, for which the best of motives is not a substitute. . . . We cannot regard the President as immune from these constitutional principles."

Unlimited power in the Executive, an Executive immune from law and free to follow the dictates of his conscience and arbitrarily to exercise his own will, even under the claim of serving the public good, is the characteristic principle of totalitarianism which fundamentally distinguishes it from Americanism. It is significant that the Supreme Court even found it necessary to reaffirm this principle. This language of the Court judicially applies that popular slogan: "In America we don't want any dictator, not even a good one." Europe failed to be saved from the "beneficent dictator" only because the dictator's claim, that he was acting in the public good, could not be resisted by a rule of law to which even he was accountable.

The N.R.A. extended the "sphere" of the "Third Economy" to bring all industry under "social discipline" by obtaining "voluntary" consent through governmental compulsion; and this power to "blue-print" industry, and to compel obedience thereto, was given entirely to the President to exercise in his discretion.   Let us pause and reflect on this in the light of the aims of the New Dealers as we have become familiar with them!   It certainly fits into the plan of their "blue-print," if not into the framework of our institutions.

The A.A.A., in its essential features, was a complete counterpart of the N.R.A.   The two Acts were complementary expressions of the same theory of the nature, scope, and function of the Federal Government.   They displayed the same total disregard for our institutions: States' rights, the division of powers in the coordinate branches of the Federal Government, and the individual rights of citizens.   The A.A.A. sought to break through State sovereignty and to vest in the Federal Government complete control over agriculture, to distort the taxing power into an instrument of regulation, and to take property away from one group of citizens and give it to another group.   No wonder the Supreme Court could not "square" this Act with the Constitution!

The N.R.A. and the A.A.A. were not merely forms of industrial and farm relief, but were actually the charter and the mechanism of wholly new concepts of our national economy—in Mr. Richberg's words "the Constitution of an economic government."

The Cotton Control Act, the Tobacco Control Act, and, last but not least, the Potato Control Act, all extended the "sphere" of the A.A.A. They illustrate that once you apply the principle of a planned economy in one situation you must of necessity extend it to all, even to hope to make its original purposes effective. All production is related, and is part of a single integrated economy. You cannot apply different economic theories and use different economic controls in each economic field. But even if this were possible, it would not suit the ambitions of the apostles of the new economy. We have seen that they *plan* the gradual extension into new fields until the "rounded whole" of the "Third Economy" is complete.

These various Acts certainly furnish a pat illustration of the detailed operation of the "Third Economy." Each called upon an all-wise central government to determine how many bales of cotton, how many pounds of tobacco, or how many bushels of potatoes, every farmer in the United States could market without the payment of a tax. These added to the basic commodities covered by the A.A.A. give a perfect picture of the Administration's farm program as the complete regimentation of all American agriculture.

Dr. Tugwell and his colleagues were progressing very rapidly toward the realization of their ideals.

The *Humphrey* case—another ghost which cast an instructive shadow—demonstrated the absolutist ambitions of our President who demanded a free hand even in removing Federal officials that held views not in sympathy with his. This savors of the "one rhythm" of Herr Hitler.

The Railroad Retirement Act attempted to establish a compulsory retirement and pension system for the employees of all carriers subject to the Interstate Commerce Act. The Supreme Court stopped this effort to manipulate our constitutional processes to serve the interests of one class at the expense of another. A few words from the Court will make the vicious implications of this seemingly humanitarian law obvious.

"Thus the Act denies due process of law by taking the property of one and bestowing it upon another This onerous financial burden cannot be justified upon the plea that it is in the interest of economy, or will promote efficiency or safety." . . .

"It is an attempt for social ends to impose by sheer fiat non-contractual incidents upon the relation of employer and employee, not as a rule or regulation of commerce and transportation between the States, but as a means of assuring a particular class of employees against old age dependency."

Government as a paternal benefactor according to its own charitable desires, and unhampered by any law, is not our American ideal of government. It has always proved the means of purchasing political surrender to a totalitarian State by promises of economic benefits. Almost every so-called social benefactor has always emulated the method of Robin Hood of robbing the rich to give to the poor. This might be the Robin Hood means to social justice, but it is not the American way. In the words of Benjamin Franklin: "Those who would give up essential liberty to purchase a little temporary safety deserve neither liberty nor safety." And he might have added: they usually eventually get neither.

To be courageous enough to state these truisms, of course, exposes one to an avalanche of invective; to be publicly damned as "anti-social," as an enemy of the poor; but it is just this lack of courage to state these truths that demagogues profit by. Each of these claims to be the one exception to his historic prototypes. Furthermore, why adopt unconstitutional methods to achieve their laudable ideals, and particularly always to select only those means which vest them with absolute power? The people have the absolute power to implement the government with any power they want. They do not need to have "their best interests" *imposed* on them by unconstitutional means and without their consent. These demagogues use every means to camouflage the political implications of their proposals. Perhaps their methods are Mr. Wallace's "psychological" arguments?

This demagogic generosity is illustrated by another ghost that walked in the night.

The Supreme Court said in the *Frazier-Lemke Act* case:

"As we conclude that the Act as applied," has taken rights in specific property which are of substantial value without compensation, and has given them to another, "we must hold it void. For the Fifth Amendment commands that, however great the nation's need, private property shall not be thus taken even for a wholly public use without just compensation."

The *Gold Clause* Cases give us a good example of constitutional immorality. The Supreme Court, although recognizing that the Government had complete jurisdiction over the monetary system, and could, therefore, render ineffective private contracts calling for payment in a type of currency which the Government could order withdrawn from circulation, nevertheless held that the Government could not lawfully repudiate its own obligations. This

decision is characteristically different from the others
we have been discussing in that the Government
was validly acting pursuant to an express constitutional grant of power—the power to coin money and
regulate the value thereof—but abused this power
by employing it to accomplish an immoral purpose—
the repudiation of its contract. It well illustrates
the doctrine of the totalitarians that the State is
unrestrained by ethical standards as well as by legal
restraints; in a word, is its own judge of its own
behavior. "The King can do no wrong," because
the King is a law unto himself. We can hear Patrick
Henry sounding down the ages: "The judiciary are
the sole protection against a tyrannical execution
the laws." Yes, even laws constitutionally enacted
can be *tyrannically* administered and applied.

As the *T.V.A.* decision has been proudly
claimed as proof of the Administration's consti-
tional righteousness, we should correctly understand
its limited meaning. The Supreme Court made
it very clear that: "We limit our decision to the case
before us, as we defined it." They said "The Wilson
Dam and its power plant must be taken to have
been constructed in the exercise of the constitutional
functions of the federal government," that is to say,
for the purpose of national defense, and for the
improvement of navigation, under federal war and
commerce powers; and also that it was constitutional

for the Federal Government to dispose of the energy
generated at the dam by government owned transmission lines. The Court did not consider that the
question as to whether or not the Federal Government could constitutionally engage in all the "col-
lateral" activities was before them for determination.
Therefore, the real implications in the activities of
the T.V.A., and its legitimate scope, still remain
to be adjudicated.

This "victory" is indeed an empty honor as far
as the real objectives of the sponsors of this project
are concerned. Whether or not it can be utilized
as a "____d-stick" to set up a rate standard for the
_____ricity, and to establish as a principle the
_____ Federal Government to itself engage in
_____ competition with private enterprise, even
_____tent of engaging in the business of manu-
_____ and selling at retail electric appliances, is
_____ be seen. We must not forget that these
_____ were claimed to be some of the expected
_____ from the T.V.A.

All of these cases are unimpeachable proof that
the Roosevelt Administration, or to be more specific,
Congress under Presidential pressure, has attempted
to inject into our statutory law, laws which are basically hostile to our governmental system. This is
not a matter of opinion, but of fact. The Supreme
Court, the final and conclusive authority on such

questions, has so determined in words that leave no room for doubt or debate. As a matter of fact, the severity of their rebuke carries with it proof of the depth of the Justices' conviction that the issues were momentous and the implications tragic. That the Supreme Court over and over again during the last few months has deemed it necessary vehemently to reassert the elemental principles of our constitutional system, especially those respecting the limiting of the powers of the Federal Government and the segregating of governmental prerogatives into different political units, is very impressive, and is apparently intended as a word of caution to the people to guard against the repeated and persistent transgressions of those dominating our government. If the Court did not profoundly feel this necessary, considerable parts of their recent decisions would be trite and would be mere phrase-mongering.

The unprecedentedly high rate of mortality of these legislative Ghosts is another evidence that some strange calamity must have visited them. It is unparalleled in our history. During the last thirty-six months, *ten* Federal laws, all signed by President Roosevelt, have been declared invalid.

During the first seventy-five years of our history, but *two* national laws were held unconstitutional by the Supreme Court, and, up until the Roosevelt Administration the number did not exceed sixty. Certainly the country was undergoing many fundamental changes in its economic and social development during the period of our country's greatest expansion. Certainly the country experienced political crises during that period. And we must bear in mind, that up to now over 24,300 public laws had been enacted. President Roosevelt, in three years, has had more of the laws he signed declared unconstitutional than did Presidents Harding, Coolidge, and Hoover in all the twelve years they were in office. And the record is still incomplete. President Roosevelt will easily attain the record of being the President of the United States who violated the Constitution more times in a single term of office than any other President of the United States in the entire past history of the country.

This is, indeed, indicative that the Administration's legislative theories are alien to our system. *But,* up to "thirty-four months" ago, we were not "writing a new chapter in the history of popular government," we were not building up "new instruments of public power" "on a broad base," we were up until then content with the constitutional instruments of public power on the fundamental base of our Constitution.

The fact that all these laws were found to have common constitutional defects cannot be attributed to mere accident, particularly when their paramount vice was the concentration of unlimited power and absolute discretion in the Executive branch of the Federal Government. The organic structure of our political system, was designed, as we have seen, with this particular vice in mind. On the other hand, this concentration of power is the basis of all the New Despotisms, and we have been repeatedly warned by our Founding Fathers and by the courts, that despotism finds its most perfect definition in the concentration of unlimited and unrestrained power in one person, or one group. That is what Despotism means. Applying this accepted definition to the findings of the Supreme Court in these cases, we can logically conclude that these laws contained the seeds of despotism in them. On the judicial record, the Administration can be justly indicted of totalitarian ambitions. At any rate, the positive trend toward this in its key measures has been recognized by our highest tribunal.

In addition, when we consider that these condemned laws were inspired, drafted, and defended by the Minor Prophets and their school, and that they so graphically carry out the "blue-print" of their "professed objectives," we have convincing proof of the direction in which the "course of the nation" is being changed. At any rate, these legislative ideas, born in the brains and nurtured in the hearts of these Utopians, were condemned as not "squaring" with Americanism.

The Ghosts of Despotism have, indeed, walked amongst us—if only for a night. And it was the distinctive principle of our political philosophy—a government of laws, not of men—enforced by the judiciary, that alone saved us. However, the mortality record is, beyond doubt, not yet complete. Some Ghosts still strut up and down the land. We should therefore, become acquainted with them, as they are recorded in our next chapter: "Some Pages from the 'new chapter in the history of popular government.'"

CHAPTER XI

THE "new chapter in the history of popular government," written by the authors of "the new instruments of public power," although severely mutilated
by the Supreme Court, as we have seen in the last
chapter, nevertheless still contain many most significant and still unedited pages, which give a very clear
picture of the whole content and substance of the
new political and economic Constitution, that they
are in process of writing chapter by chapter. While
each page at first reading might appear to be an
entirely separate episode, yet, on careful scrutiny, we
find that they are in fact perfectly coherent and progressive instalments of a single theme. We should,
therefore, select at random and studiously re-read
some of these pages. We should also try to read
between the lines, for, perhaps, some obscure or
concealed meaning.

These pages will illustrate the "new instruments of
public power" in action and will show how they have
been used to transform our system of government, to

encroach upon the guaranteed liberties of individuals, and to advance the consummation of the "New Order."

In spite of the obstacles cast in their way by the Supreme Court, the authors of this "new chapter" have not retreated from their chosen course, but with renewed determination have returned to the attack with the same constitutional armaments.

The Administration forced the passing of the Guffey Coal Act. This Act attempts to apply the same kind of governmental control over *one* industry as the Supreme Court condemned in respect of *all* industry by the attempted use of the same constitutional processes condemned in the *Schechter* case. To extend Federal jurisdiction over an industry by imposing "voluntary" compliance by coercive penalties under the pretended use of the taxing power clearly shows the extent to which a constitutional pretext will be seized upon to attain indirectly objectives not having any expressed sanction. The economic soundness of this Act has been questioned by some of the leaders of the industry itself. As to its constitutionality the Administration itself has confessed some doubts. Perhaps the sponsors of the Act were influenced by some political motives. Perhaps they hoped it would serve as another illustration to the people that the Constitution is inadequate to meet present economic conditions.

The National Labor Relations Act also tries to utilize the same constitutional processes in the field of industrial relations, to the extent of even interfering with the freedom of contract between employers and their employees as to hours of work, wages, and conditions of labor.

The Securities and Exchange Act, not only attempts the Federal control of all securities markets, but, by asserting jurisdiction over the stock exchanges as alleged instrumentalities of interstate commerce, reaches into the field not only of the regulation but also of the prescription of corporate and financial practices and accounting methods of private enterprises, many of which are wholly intrastate in their activities. It goes even further and asserts control over credit and over the stock holdings of individuals.

The Public Utility Holding Company Act sets up even greater controls in another field, and not only seeks similar regulation of corporate and financial practices but, in some respects, also tries to pass upon the "economical and efficient operation" of the business itself. Practically every activity of a public utility holding company, including service, sales, and construction contracts, is put under direct governmental control even to the extent of giving an agency of the government the power to determine whether certain public utility systems should be allowed to continue in existence.

The Securities and Exchange Act, and the Public Utility Holding Company Act, were proposed as needed reforms of abuses and malpractices and for the necessary protection of the public, but, as finally enacted, they far exceeded any such specific and worthy purposes and extended the "spheres" of governmental activities into a rather complete management of private enterprises. They are not merely regulatory; they are, in fact, managerial. Whether constitutional or not, they certainly fulfill many of the "professed objectives" of the Minor Prophets by the methods of the "Third Economy," as proposed by Dr. Tugwell in his California speech. As specifications of the "blue-print" of "social economy," they are very illuminating.

Other legislative examples of constitutional distortions might be cited, but for the fact that it would only be repetitious monotony, as those considered are adequate to substantiate the claim that the legislative endeavors of the Administration demonstrate an earnest effort to fit entirely new economic and social theories into the framework of our political institutions, and that those efforts all have a totalitarian trend.

These Prophets, however, display a phenomenal perseverance and determination, an almost indefatigable stubbornness, to carry out their "professed objectives," in spite of even severe judicial rebuke.

Almost immediately after the Supreme Court nullified the Frazier-Lemke Act, the Railroad Retirement Act, and the Agricultural Adjustment Act, they caused basically similar legislation to be introduced and enacted by Congress. Modifications to dodge the original constitutional objections are, of course, used, but the basic theories and objectives of the original laws are substantially reasserted. They pay a lip-service to the Constitution, but feel confident that "lawyers and statesmen may eventually find a way" to evade it, "by modifying the proposal somewhat," as Dr. Ezekiel advises. It is the substance of their economic and social ideals which are of paramount importance to them, not our political ideals of freedom.

They best illustrate their firm determination to accomplish their purposes, regardless of the cost to individual rights, by their attempts to deprive the individual citizen of his means of obtaining judicial protection.

After the *Gold Clause* decision, they promptly obtained legislation shutting off suits, after January 1st, 1936, by holders of Federal securities who claim specific damages by virtue of the devaluation of the dollar. Having been found guilty of an immoral act, they rushed to make themselves immune and unaccountable for its commission.

Somewhat similar action was taken by the Administration in the amendments to the A.A.A., which made it practically impossible to recover processing taxes, even though these were illegally and unconstitutionally collected. And the citizen was deprived by these amendments of his right to protect himself by injunction, as injunctions against the collection of the tax were forbidden.

The violence of their distemper reached its climax in the most amazing statement made by the Secretary of Agriculture in respect to the Supreme Court's ordering the return of impounded processing taxes. He said: "This is probably the greatest legalized steal in American history." The lack of restraint, the utter abandon, of this statement surpasses all understanding, and makes one terrified at the recklessness with which these innovators defy existing authority. President Roosevelt, in his running remarks at his conference with the press after the N.R.A. decision, displayed a somewhat similar, although a more restrained, distemper at this judicial check-mating of his desires. This impatience with restraint is a psychological characteristic of all who have the obsession for personal power.

All of these laws, the propriety of which we have here questioned, those wiped from our statute books as well as those which remain at least for the time being, strikingly demonstrate that the fundamental principles of our Constitution are at stake—

not merely meaningless technicalities. They prove a consistent purpose to destroy the essential features, and to transform the organic structure of our government. We must not be lulled into the acceptance of these modifications under the mistaken belief that they are purely jurisdictional adaptations and readjustments of procedure to meet new economic and social demands. On the contrary, they are direct efforts to break down the protection, which we have seen that the structure of our government affords to the vital principles of our institutions. These laws certainly create a "new relationship between government and people" as we understood that relationship up until "thirty-four months" ago.

It seems to us, that when considered collectively, all these queer-shaped pieces of legislation fit together as a jigsaw puzzle picture which depicts a highly centralized government with such power concentrated in its executive branch, as to give it the appearance, if not the substance, of a totalitarian State. This design or pattern of government was discarded by our Founding Fathers when they devised our Constitution, has been consistently challenged by the Supreme Court whenever presented with any tendency toward its establishment, and has been without exception repudiated by the American people on every occasion when it has been offered them.

But the pages of this "new chapter in the history of

popular government" record even more incidents of the concentration of power in the hands of the Executive!

All legislative powers are vested in Congress. The President may, however, *recommend* for the consideration of Congress such measures as he shall judge necessary and expedient; and he has the power of veto over laws passed by Congress, but Congress can, of course, over-ride his veto.

This narrowly circumscribed power to participate in the enactment of laws has been recently distorted into practically extending the Executive power to such limits as to absorb the independence of the legislature. President Roosevelt has had most of the key legislation of his Administration drafted outside of the halls of Congress by "expert draftsmen" planted in various executive agencies, and has had these bills, thus drafted, introduced into Congress by Administration "whips," who in some instances do not even thoroughly understand the bill which they introduce and which bears their name. Perfunctory public hearings, and often no public hearings at all, are held. The bill is included in the President's list of "must" legislation and is passed by an overwhelming Democratic Congress which fears to show any public refusal to obey the President's "must." In practical effect, the Executive initiates and enacts such legislation, and the action of Congress is purely formal.

The very characterization of proposed legislation as *"must"* legislation, portrays a complete misconception of, and disrespect for, our constitutional separation of governmental functions. This recalls to our minds Hitler's statement that: "But neither Senate nor Chamber shall have power to make decisions; they are appointed to work and not to make decisions. . . . That is the exclusive prerogative of the responsible President for the time being." And let us not forget that it is the branch of the Government, which the Founding Fathers designed as the one to be expressive of the independent will of the people, that is now dominated and absorbed by the Executive. This is certainly totalitarian in its consequences.

We must not be unmindful of the political power which was vested in the President by placing $4,880,000,000 (to mention only one item) in his hands to be expended at his absolute discretion. No single governmental unit in the United States has been given the power to levy taxes and to appropriate public funds. These acts require the coordinate actions of both Houses of Congress and of the Executive—each supposedly acting independently of, and as a check on, the other. To give to the President that amount of money, without any detailed designation of its use, is not "appropriation"; it is, practically, giving him a blank check. Congress has the right, and the duty, to specify the purposes for which public funds shall be used. The fact that expenditures of general treasury funds cannot be challenged by a taxpayer is a mere technicality, and does not excuse the violation of the spirit of the constitutional provision. On the contrary, it imposes a higher moral duty on any governmental official respectful of his fiduciary obligation.

How can an Administration, so suspicious of concentrated wealth as President Roosevelt's pretends to be, justify its Executive's spending so much money in his absolute and unreviewable discretion? Especially how can this be done by an Administration which constantly indicts the concentration of wealth as being an instrument of political power, and as being destructive of popular government and of individual freedom. Is not popular government and individual freedom just as much endangered by such a concentration of money in the hands of an unaccountable sovereign as in the hands of any private person? That question has been conclusively answered by the history of all governments. "He who holds the purse-strings rules the realm." Certainly our Founding Fathers did not trust any such power in the Executive Branch of our Government.

Does history prove that only private persons, and never sovereigns, have misused the power of money? The Administration, therefore, must make its claim of immunity from the dangers of the concentration of wealth in its own hands on the theory that no one is to be trusted but itself. Surely, this is totalitarian in its conception.

Like all crusaders, those directing and controlling the policy of the present Administration are so obsessed with the conviction that they alone have the "way to salvation" that they become impatient with, and intolerant of, any and all opposition. They resolve to destroy it by the "sword" if necessary. We have observed that this is a common characteristic of the leaders of the New Despotisms and, in fact, of all historic dictators.

Now, tolerance is absolutely essential to democracy. Democracy being the expression of the popular will in political action the expression must be free and untrammeled; must be encouraged and stimulated; must not be suppressed. The full expression of opinion is a vital function of democracy and is the strongest obstacle to dictatorship. Popular expression is the means by which the common denominator of public opinion can be ascertained; that common denominator, when obtained, is majority opinion. If through intolerance, we deny or forbid the expression of opinion, we thereby prevent the true ascertainment of majority opinion, by excluding the opinions of some persons. Therefore, an opinion, so ascertained, is not the opinion of the majority, but only that of those permitted to express their opinion; and to all others it is an *imposed* opinion. Thus an essential feature of democracy is destroyed. We have already seen that intolerance is the prelude to the suppression of opposition, and that the elimination of opposition means "one party, one pattern, one rhythm, one creed"; the ultimate, the inevitable, the necessary, objective of every totalitarian.

There are in this country already marked evidences of intolerance. Those who have the courage openly to oppose the present regime, or even critically to comment on any of its activities, are denounced in vituperative language as being public enemies. These denunciations come from those in the highest governmental positions, and when they are speaking in their official capacity. The floors of Congress are thus desecrated. Congressional immunity is used as a protective cloak. Investigations, conducted at public expense and under the pretext of obtaining information to assist Congress in legislating, are converted into "fishing expeditions" for evidence useful only to discredit an individual or class, and for the purpose of stirring up popular animosities, and are quite common. In some of these "investigations," the rules of evidence and of procedure, both of which are designed to protect individual rights, are totally disregarded. The "investigator" is prosecutor, judge, and jury.

Recently a Special Committee of the Senate, acting under a Senate resolution authorizing it to investigate certain alleged "lobbying" activities, singled out certain organizations and individuals, who were reputed to be critical of certain legislation, and ordered all telegrams, sent or received by them for many months, to be seized. No one of those favorable to the legislation in question, regardless of his "lobbying" or other activities, was subjected to this injustice and indignity. No distinction was made as to communications between attorneys and clients, and between husband and wife, both of which are sacred and privileged in every court of law; nor was any regard paid to the pertinency of the communications to the subject-matter of the inquiry. It has been estimated that several millions of private messages have been examined by this Senate Committee.

"The protection of papers," according to a judicial decision, "is as much secured under the provisions of the Bill of Rights as a man's house, and the same rules that apply to one apply to the other." Another court has said: "Give such a body, in addition, the power to search any man's papers for evidence . . . and you convert it into a tribunal which would soon become as odius to American citizens as the Star Chamber was to Englishmen, or the Spanish inquisition to the civilized world." The Fourth Amendment, guaranteeing that the right of the people to be secure in their persons, houses, papers, and effects, from unreasonable searches and seizures, shall not be violated, seemed to be no obstacle in the minds of these Senatorial inquisitors.

As an aggravating circumstance, an agency of the Executive Department collaborated with this Special Committee of the Senate in seizing these telegrams, even though "lobbying" in any sense of the word does not come within the statutory functions of this agency. The Federal Communications Commission is a part of the Executive Branch of the government, an independent commission answerable only to the President. It is the President's personal agent. In other words, the Executive Branch, without authority, lent itself to the request of a Senatorial Committee to secure through subterfuge for that Committee information which the Committee had not been able to secure itself. It is reliably estimated that over 13,000 messages were inspected by the Federal Communications Commission, and copies of these were made and turned over to the Senate Committee. This is a good illustration of legislative and executive agencies' disregarding their constitutional separation and combining against the individual, and of their attempting to substitute their will for law.

There are literally millions of confidential messages passing over the leased wires of the important newspapers and press associations every year and other millions are sent and received by papers which utilize the regular commercial wires of the telegraph companies. These messages are an integral part of the mechanics of a free press. There is already an instance of such communications being seized.

This whole revolting revelation is a striking instance of what is happening in many countries but what we thought we were protected from.

When "lobbying" becomes lobbying in the invidious sense of that word, and ceases to be simply the right of petition guaranteed by the Constitution, is, of course, a serious question, but apparently the distinction between these two aspects of lobbying is now drawn solely on the principle as to whether or not the "activities" were friendly or unfriendly to the inquirer. The investigator was just hunting in the hopes of finding something which he might utilize against those being investigated. This has the appearance not of lobbying *before* Congress, but of lobbying *by* Congress.

The Chairman of this Special Committee offered as a justification that it was necessary to seize these telegrams to prevent the possibility of their being burned, as had once occurred. This is equivalent to saying that in order to prevent a person from burning his own private telegrams the Constitution should be burned. To use the language of the Supreme Court, this would seem to argue that the Senate "intended to authorize one of its agencies to sweep all our traditions into the fire, and to direct fishing expeditions into private papers on the possibility that they might disclose" evidence pertinent to the matter under investigation.

Even the right and sworn duty of lawyers to support, maintain, and defend the Constitution, through their constitutional right of free speech, has been challenged. They have even had their professional integrity questioned because they have dared publicly to express an opinion on constitutional issues. The administrators of this "New Order" become true to type and grow intolerant of all criticism. To question their infallibility is heresy.

Voluminous questionnaires and interrogatories of the most detailed and private character, requiring answer under oath and under pain of penalty, are received almost daily from executive agencies. Most of the information ordered to be given can be of little, if indeed any, public use. Considerable of this information is published for the use of competitors, the entertainment of idle gossipers, and, in some instances, as a punitive weapon. Apparently all business has become "vested with a public interest." One reads with a smile the following words of a judicial opinion, wondering if they can possibly apply to our country at the present time: "The natural law of privacy in one's own affairs which exists in liberty loving peoples and nations . . . for no right is more vital to 'liberty and the pursuit of happiness' than the protection of the citizen's private affairs, their right to be let alone."

But we must not extend our pages from the "new chapter in the history of popular government" to inordinate length, although it would take a sizeable volume to do them justice. The pages we have here selected are sufficient to show the trend away from our traditional conduct and into alien paths, all of which lead to the ultimate destination—dictatorship. Before, however, concluding our examination of the record made in this respect by the present Administration, we shall devote a short chapter to a summary study of the progress the New Deal has already achieved in establishing the most extensive Bureaucracy which has ever existed.

CHAPTER XII

NEW DEAL BUREAUCRACY

WE HAVE seen that this apparently limitless political control, extending over practically all social and economic activity, has been, and is planned to be, concentrated in the Executive.

Much of the recent legislation is more in the nature of a general legislative declaration of broad principles, policies, and theories, with a delegation to the Executive of the most comprehensive power to determine its specific application and the manner of its use; instead of our traditional pattern of legislation, which gives a complete, detailed, and specific expression of the legislative will and entrusts the Executive only with its enforcement and with its administration. In some recent instances it has even been left optional with the President whether or not the law should ever become operative. Furthermore, many of these recent enactments, on their face, evidence an Executive absorption of legislative functions and constitute complete abdication of Congress in favor of the President. Obviously, a certain amount of administrative discretion must be allowed the enforcing officer to assure an efficient execution of a law according to its true purport; but there is a sharp differentiation between administrative discretion and legislative power. The so-called "administrative discretion" under much New Deal legislation is so comprehensive and absolute as to include for all practical purposes the power of determining whether or not and under what conditions, the law shall become operative, the power of defining its scope, and of interpreting and construing its meaning, and the power of prescribing the mechanics for its enforcement, by decrees, orders, rules and regulations. The power thus attempted to be transferred to the Executive clearly transcends all our previous notions of "administration" and resembles, if indeed it is not in fact, "law-making." We have seen that the Supreme Court has already taken this view most unequivocally in several cases involving such laws.

In addition, the Executive is given power to punish infractions of these laws, as well as violations of his own self-promulgated orders, rules, and regulations. The proceedings to enforce these penalties are conducted by "administrative" bodies as executives agencies, and the "administrators" act as prosecutor, judge and jury. Many of the protections afforded by judicial procedure are denied. We are told that this is merely augmenting our judicial system with what is termed "administrative law."

Now, there is a fundamental difference between "administrative law" and the executive absorption of judicial prerogatives. To confuse them may readily lead to our losing our judicial protection against executive oppression by leaving us at the mercy of agencies appointed and controlled by the Executive, for the adjudication of our rights. History records many sad and tragic examples of this practice.

History has taught us that the protection of our liberty requires that the legislative branch—the people's branch of the government—must be the one which prescribes crimes and misdemeanors and fixes punishment and penalities for their commission. To make it a punishable offense to violate rules, regulations, and decrees of an Executive—some of which are so general in their language as not to make clear in advance what constitutes prohibited action —places the citizen, if not in jeopardy of punishment at Executive will, at least, under the terror of acting at his peril in many instances where he cannot reasonably inform himself in advance of consequences of his action. If freedom is to prevail, the criminal law, under which man may be deprived of his personal liberty, cannot reside in the Executive conscience.

Even if these extremes have not been reached, we note a mild beginning and a strong tendency in that direction. We have observed instances where citizens, even under the advice of counsel, have entertained such apprehensions with considerable justification.

Decrees, orders, rules, and regulations, flow from these many executive agencies in such quantity that it is impossible for a citizen to keep up with the "laws" which he is bound to obey, if indeed, he is sufficiently fortunate to be able even to find out whether they exist. The N.R.A. alone put out over 10,000 pages of pronouncements, supposedly having the effect of law, in one year—"a total which greatly exceeds the volume of all Federal Statutes now in effect." This quotation is from the Committee on Administrative Law of the American Bar Association which also stated that the "judicial branch of the Federal government is being rapidly and seriously undermined," and that these New Deal agencies "are obliterating essential lines of our government structure and substituting a labyrinth in which the rights of individuals, while preserved in form, can easily be nullified in practise," and as a result "it becomes hopeless for the average citizen to understand his government."

The Supreme Court itself felt constrained to ask the Department of Justice for a list of all New Deal orders, rules, and regulations, that have the force of law. Up until now there is no such list available. In plain words, nobody has this information at his command or for his use.

Now, of necessity, the Executive can only perform the multitudinous functions required of him by these manifold activities of the New Deal through commissions, boards, councils, departments and agencies, most of the members of which he appoints without the advice and consent of the Senate, and who, in ever-increasing numbers, are free from the restrictions of the civil service laws. He is practically compelled to delegate most of the "administrative discretion."

The President, who had pledged himself to drastic reduction in the number of government agencies and employees, more than doubled the number of governmental agencies, in fact, set up more new ones than the total number set up in all the one hundred forty-four previous years of our government. It would only be tiresome reiteration to give a detailed enumeration of all those new agencies with their alphabetical designations in almost every possible combination of three and four letters. These bureaucrats are housed in one hundred and one government-owned and one hundred and three leased buildings in the City of Washington, not to mention all the offices occupied by them throughout the entire country. No other government capital, no other age, ever witnessed an expansion of bureaucracy such as Washington has seen in the last three years.

Prior to 1933, in the Administration, which, according to Candidate Roosevelt was more extravagant than any previous peace-time government of history, the total number of employees of all executive and governmental agencies was 600,000. This, according to the most conservative estimates, has been increased by 190,000—to 790,000. President Roosevelt, who professed during his campaign to have such a clear picture of the immediate emergencies and the action required to meet them, could hardly have been so mistaken in his estimated requirements as sincerely to promise a drastic cut and then to give us such a tremendous increase. At best this is a serious misjudgment and mis-appraisal of the situation.

To these must be added literally millions of persons who are more or less dependent upon the largess of the government. No city or community throughout the entire country is forgotten in this wholesale distribution of Federal favors. No city or community is left unaffected by Federal activities of one kind or another. Local authorities are provoked to extravagance by the ambitions of their constituents not to be treated less generously than others in their Federal benefits. State and local governments have been tempted to sacrifice their rights and forsake their responsibility in order to get a share of Federal funds. The Federal Government becomes of paramount importance in the eyes of the people. Local independence and the local pride in self-helpfulness is impaired. The sense of local responsibility is destroyed. Local self-government, one of the institutions of our government, is thereby broken down and becomes merged into one great centralized Federal Government. This changes the whole complexion of our governmental system.

A general classification of these governmental agencies will bring to our minds a realization of how they have reached into almost every conceivable field of human endeavor; control over prices, wages, working conditions, production, distribution, transportation, and over commercial and competitive practices, in all industries and agriculture; the promotion and development of manufacturing; slum clearance and housing; general banking, mortgage and farm mortgage loans, chattel mortgage loans, farm credits, saving and international banking; insurance and underwriting; control of stock exchanges and securities markets and the distribution of securities; general real estate; trading in agricultural commodities; control over public utility operations in all phases, including the manufacture and retail sales of electrical appliances and the acquisition and operation of retail distribution of electrical energy in competition with private enterprise; every variety of emergency relief directly conducted by the Federal Government or indirectly by means of Federal contributions to the States and municipalities; operas, musicals, theatricals and other cultural endeavors. This is certainly a "fairly rounded whole."

Some governmental bureaus and agencies are, of course, necessary mechanisms in the operation of government. Where these are purely administrative assistances they must be condoned as necessary evils; but, on the other hand, when they transgress administrative functions and assume legislative and judicial prerogatives, they should be viewed with alarm. Our system of distributed powers was designed to prohibit this, and to prevent the disproportionate growth of one branch of government at the expense of the others. Bureaucracy, having the powers and discretion transferred to it from the constitutional departments of the Government, such as we have observed under the New Deal, results in a fundamental alteration in the very structure of our Government. Whether this is necessary or advisable, even under emergency conditions, might be debatable, but we should at least be conscious of its political import. Also, what assurance have we that these "temporary" usurpations will not prove permanent?

And we must not forget that the Democratic Platform of 1932, which the President solemnly declared was a covenant with the people, provided that relief was the obligation of the State and local governments. After three years of experimentation relief is still necessary, so that the emergency measures dedicated to emergency relief seem to have failed of one of their principal avowed objectives of getting people back to normal employment. It cannot be denied that this was one of the primary purposes of the particular kind of relief measures adopted as its sponsors committed themselves to this claim. Apparently, the methods adopted have not fulfilled all that was claimed for them. The tragedy is not only that their methods have caused a breakdown in local self-government, but also, as a high official recently observed, the "people have come to consider relief as something natural." The old horror of living on the town seems to have disappeared from the minds of many people. Now, let us not be misunderstood. We earnestly advocate necessary and provident relief, but we challenge the soundness of the methods pursued by the New Dealers. Their methods savor of political nepotism, or, perhaps, they are indulging themselves in a paternalistic orgy. And what will happen when all these relief benefits are stopped?

James M. Beck, in his excellent volume "Our Wonderland of Bureaucracy," written before the recent remarkable growth of bureaucracy under the present Administration, gives us an excellent definition of bureaucracy. "Bureaucracy" has two meanings, he says. As an invidious term, it "primarily refers in a democratic government to the aggrandizement of the Executive at the expense of the Legislative Branch of the government. This refers only to the mechanics of a government. . . . In a broader sense, bureaucracy refers to the irrepressible war between the individual and the State, and involves the question as to the just limits, under the higher law, of the State over the property and life of the individual." That concisely states the inevitable consequences of bureaucracy to which there is no single exception in history. It is the natural development from government by the personal will of men.

In the words of John W. Davis: "If experience teaches anything it is that of all methods of Government, bureaucracy is the least responsible, the least intelligent, and the most arrogant and tyrannical. It is the nature of bureaucracy that responsibility is widely diffused, decision is anonymous, and action painfully slow. . . . Once the halting, blundering hand of the bureaucrat has settled down on an industry or a country, a creeping paralysis sets in that betokens the end of growth or even of life itself." Nothing could better state the universal experience with bureaucracy.

Now, this bureaucracy of such staggering proportions, and with such extraordinary powers and vaunting ambitions, is the logical and customary outgrowth of the concentration of so much power in one branch of the government. It is an inevitable and inherent attribute of every highly centralized form of government. Individual freedom is submerged in this flood of officialdom. Self-government becomes diluted by mass-government. The integrity of the individual is trampled upon by the organized mob of government agents.

We soon discover who the "forgotten man" really is. He is the citizen who dares to assert his inalienable right to liberty against the will of the government. If the "forgotten man," originally made the subject of such solicitous care by the New Deal, were the citizen who did not receive his equitable share of wealth and opportunity in the economic order of our society, he has certainly evolved into the citizen, who, perhaps, economically remembered is now politically forgotten. Political liberty is just as much an essential ingredient of freedom as is economic security. Man cannot live by bread alone.

It is pure sophistry to attempt to differentiate between economic autocracy and political autocracy in their effects upon individual liberties. An economic autocracy is always subject to what has been so picturesquely described as "the law of the tooth and the claw," so that economic autocracy can never become absolute because of the competitive and different interests of those having any substantial economic interest. Under political control of economics the natural restraining influence of competition between different interests is removed, and all are regimented under a single control, and therefore we have an absolute economic as well as a political autocracy. On the one hand, the Government already has adequate powers under the anti-monopoly laws to combat all unreasonable efforts of monopolistic economic control, and the failure of the Government to exercise these powers is no reason why it should ask for greater power. On the other hand, there is no protection against the concentration of power in a political autocracy *except* the Constitution. It is significant to observe that "the apostles of economic greed" are not preaching the repeal of the anti-monopoly laws, but the authors of the "new chapters in the history of popular government" are challenging the Constitution. To combat economic autocracy by setting up a political autocracy is simply transferring us from one dictator to another, and of the two, political dictatorship is the more to be feared, particularly as in all of its historic prototypes it includes economic dictatorship.

It is in all probability for these reasons that the New Dealers dazzle our minds with the horrors of economic autocracy so as to prevent us from perceiving their gradual setting up of a political autocracy.

It would take volumes to give a complete and statistical picture of the ramifications of the workings of the bureaucracy set up in the last three years.

It is our sole purpose, however, to observe the fact that such a bureaucracy is being built up and to understand its political consequences. We are not concerned with the details but only with the political principles involved.

A striking proof of the fact that the Roosevelt bureaucracy, like all its prototypes, has already assumed an autocratic authority antagonistic to our constitutional concepts, with the inevitable consequence of trespassing upon individual liberty, is furnished by the *Jones* case just decided by the Supreme Court of the United States. In that case the Supreme Court was called upon to scrutinize certain administrative atcivities of the Securities and Exchange Commission. The Court apparently considered that the circumstances required the use of extraordinarily severe language, as it said:

"The action of the Commission finds no support in right, principle or in law. It is wholly unreasonable and arbitrary. It violates the cardinal precept upon which the constitutional safeguards of personal liberty ultimately rests, that this shall be a government of laws, because to the precise extent that the mere will of an official or an official body is permitted to take the place of allowable official discretion or to supplant the standing law as a rule of human conduct. The government ceases to be one of laws and becomes an autocracy. . . .

"Arbitrary power and the rule of the Constitution cannot both exist. They are antagonistic and incompatible forces; and one or the other must of necessity perish whenever they are brought into conflict.

"To borrow the words of Mr. Justice Day: 'There is no place in our constitutional system for the exercise of arbitrary power.' Garfield versus Goldsby, 211 U S 249, 262. To escape assumptions of such power on the part of the three primary departments of the government, is not enough. Our institutions must be kept free from the appropriation of unauthorized power by lesser agencies as well.

"And if the various administrative bureaus and commissions, necessarily called and being called into existence by the increasing complexities of our modern business and political affairs, are permitted gradually to extend their powers by encroachments, even petty encroachments, upon the fundamental rights, privileges and immunities of the people, we shall in the end, while avoiding the fatal consequences of a supreme autocracy, become submerged by a multitude of minor invasions of personal rights, less destructive but no less violative of constitutional guarantees."

The panorama of bureaucracy, which we have given, should suffice conclusively to demonstrate the consequences of personal government in the working. We observe not only a concentration of power in the hands of the Executive but also an absorption by the Executive of the legislative and judicial branches of the Government. We have in fact progressed far, so far, indeed, that Americanism is now at the Crossroads.

CHAPTER XIII

AMERICANISM AT THE CROSSROADS

NATIONS are built out of philosophy, not out of bricks and mortar. It is their national ideals which shape their national destinies. It is their popular thinking which determines their ideas of the political nature, rights, and ambitions of the individual. Economic and social forces and circumstances obviously play a vital part in man's existence, particularly in determining the measure of his creature comforts and in providing for his material well-being, but he is not a mere robot completely and exclusively controlled by them. He is given power over nature; that is his divine heritage and is what makes him a MAN.

The church edifice does not prescribe the religion; the religion prescribes and produces the edifice. So with our political structure. It is built with political ideals and ideas. Our ideal is to have a social and economic structure in a framework in which freedom can live. We should encourage and stimulate every improvement and betterment in our economic and social order, but because we have detected some failures or imperfections in our past economic system does not even imply that we should destroy all the ideals of our civilization. There is no need to commit constitutional suicide in the hope of an economic reincarnation.

Our Constitution, as we have seen, is the Charter of our national ideals. It contains within its four corners the characteristic principles of our political philosophy. These principles are not sterile epigrams; they are living, moving, vital, forces. We do not contend that the Constitution is an untouchable sacred document. We do, however, emphatically maintain, that, in addition to prescribing a popular and efficient mechanical system of government, it also formalizes and vitalizes a distinct political philosophy—Americanism—and that the right of the people to determine the form and character of their government is a sacred, an untouchable, right. If the Constitution should need to be made more nearly perfect in order to fulfill its philosophy in changed conditions, we should proceed to such perfecting in conformity with the prescribed constitutional process of amendment. It is not necessary to scrap, or to evade, the fundamental theory of democracy by denying the people their sovereign right to consent to the kind of government by which they desire to be governed, through indirect means and under the alluring pretext of adaptation.

Proposed amendments must be carefully scrutinized, however, for there can be amendments, which are dedicated not only to adapt our *form* of government to new and unforeseen situations, but also those which completely destroy or change our fundamental and traditional political philosophy, and result in the establishment of an entirely different theory of government. The distinction between the two is fundamental. We must carefully weigh each proposal to see in which class it falls.

One class of such proposed amendments is adaptation: the other is nullification. One is reform: the other revolution.

There is no doubt that efforts to extend the scope of Federal power under the Constitution have been made throughout our national life, and that the scope of the Constitution has already been greatly expanded by judicial interpretation. But these expansions, as determined by the courts, were kept within the framework of our Federal system. There is, however, no single period in our history when so many and such far-reaching expansions were attempted; expansions which "obliterated" the Federal system, and endeavored to extend Federal jurisdiction over every conceivable social and economic activity. The very principle and nature of these recent efforts demonstrate, beyond peradventure of doubt, that the present Administration is intent upon fundamentally changing our constitutional order. Certainly, the Administration should realize by now that it cannot consummate its program by "interpretation." Its policies will not fit into the scheme of our Government. Nevertheless, the Administration still persists, in spite of all obstacles, which is very significant.

It is no adequate answer to say that the constitutional processes of amendment move too slowly. The Constitution has been amended twenty-one times, and the last time the process was completed with a rapidity which conclusively proves how amenable to amendment it is when the public demand is clear.

Moreover, the contention is made that extraordinary and emergency conditions, such as have existed for the past few years, can only be effectively met by the concentration of the most comprehensive, if not absolute, powers in the Executive, and that our constitutional restrictions hamper us in coping with these problems. The recent experience of Europe under practically the same general conditions does not support this opinion. It is not in the totalitarian States in Europe that economic depression has been most effectively combated and that the greatest gains have been made. England and the Scandinavian countries, where economic liberalism still survives, are today the most prosperous in Europe.

Nothing could better illustrate the fundamental hostility in philosophical thinking between the authors of the Constitution and the authors of the "new chapter in the history of popular government" than synthetically to sum up their respective teachings, as we have observed them at length. The Founding Fathers were realists. They isolated the very germ of practical freedom from philosophical abstractions. The Prophets of the New Deal, on the other hand, have no sense of the realities; they are pure theorists. They speak of economic freedom theoretically, but when, as we have discovered from their own activities, their ideas are given a practical application they prove to be regimentation. The Founding Fathers strove to equalize individual opportunity and enterprise; the Prophets of the New Deal destroy individual opportunity and enterprise by causing *all* opportunity and enterprise to be absorbed by the State, and by causing each individual to have his share meted out to him by the State. The Founding Fathers liberated the mind: the new Prophets destroy the independence of the mind. Under our Founding Fathers each citizen drew his own design of life: under the Prophets of the New Deal, the design is drawn for him, and he merely traces the pattern given him. He executes the orders from above. One frees Man: the other enslaves him. Human life is given a new valuation, and the fundamental meaning of values has been changed. Therein lies the fundamental difference between Americanism and the Totalitarian State. It is simply the difference in belief as to whether the State is the creature of Man, or, if Man be the creature of the State: whether the State be the master or is the servant of the citizen.

The State is not a mystical, metaphysical person, having an individuality all its own and entirely independent of the citizens which compose it, as the totalitarians would have us believe; it is simply an aggregation of individuals conveniently associated for the purpose of better working out their collective and common civil interests. The idea that the administrators of the State cease to be mere men, and take on some divine, infallible nature immediately upon their assuming power and continuing only as long as they themselves remain in power, is a totalitarian fantasy; but this is an absolutely indispensable premise to justify their activities.

We have seen that the old struggle between arbitrary government by men and government by law; that is, the ancient contention between government by personal law and government by impersonal law, based on natural, constitutional, and statutory law to which man's opinion is subordinated, has been renewed today. This is purely a new version of an old historic issue. John W. Davis has wisely epitomized this historical truism when he observed: "For liberty, it has been well said, is possible only when the sovereign power is made to obey the law."

Under various guises and disguises,—Fascism in Italy, Nazism in Germany, and Sovietism in Russia—the will of the individual agent of the government has been substituted for the established written law which binds all: the officials of the government as well as the private citizen.

One of the inner circle, himself, observed this same dictatorial trend in the United States, for General Johnson said: "Thus with a few facts, little experience and no other rule than trial and error, we have submitted our economic system—prices, trading, agriculture, the value of savings and the buying power of salaries and wages—to administrative will. If that isn't dictatorship, what is it?"

We have made it very clear that our Government was not only established as one of impersonal law, but also that its Founders planned it to place certain individual rights forever above and beyond the reach of government, or of even a majority of the people as is the case in a pure democracy, and every precaution was taken in the written instrument of its foundation to safeguard these rights from usurpation or encroachment by the government, by depriving it of the power ever to become dangerous. We have seen from the record that the tendency, and, in fact, the positive efforts, of the New Dealers, are to escape from these restraints and to lodge increasing power in the Executive, and to liberate him as far as possible from legal accountability. Today there is even a widespread fear of government and a feeling that it is hopeless to fight against an adverse decision of a government official, if, indeed, one ever has the courage to initiate such a fight.

These efforts to penetrate our constitutional barriers by "obliterating" the States, and by breaking down the division of governmental functions, in a word, by attempting to lodge unlimited and untrammeled power in the Executive Department, have progressed so far that the Supreme Court has had repeated occasion to administer stinging rebukes and to sound clear and dogmatic words of warning. These tendencies in our political "progress" are no longer questions of opinion. They are determined and adjudicated facts. We have been judicially told, even though it should have been self-evident to us from the record, that this tampering with the organic structure of our government results in depriving us of the enjoyment of those inalienable rights, and of rights of self-government, which are essential to our freedom.

It cannot be the exaggeration of an alarmist to contend, with this record before us, that those at present officially controlling our national policies and directing our governmental activities, are strenuously advocating political ideals and using "new instruments of public power," which are impregnating our national life with totalitarian tendencies. They are supplying a directive force which can so change the minds of the people as to change the whole nation's course. They have confused, if not distorted, our traditional democratic ideas, and have tinkered with, if not deliberately tried to destroy, our constitutional processes, in their endeavors to stamp their political philosophy on our institutions.

The technique by which they attempt to impose their "professed objectives" has already been condemned as unconstitutional, and for them publicly to challenge all constitutional restraints displays their adherence to the totalitarian doctrine of a government of personal laws: to the will of man.

We have demonstrated that our Constitution is a solemn compact or contract between the government and the people, reserving to the people certain God-given inalienable rights and granting the government certain limited powers to provide the means for the fullest enjoyment of those rights consonant with the general welfare. If this contract requires modification to make it more conducive to the good of all, one party—the government—should not attempt, or even assume, to impose such a modification without the consent of the other party—the people—; or to maneuver the people into a position where they have unknowingly and irrevocably committed themselves to such changes. The fair thing to do is to ask for the changes and let the people decide for themselves if they wish to accept or to reject them. That is the constitutional method of amendment.

The conduct of those at the present time executing this contract on the one part, discloses that that party —the government—*either* does not understand the letter and the spirit of its contract; *or,* understanding it, does not intend to respect it; or else purposes to modify it without the express consent of the other party—the people—; or in fact without even disclosing the change to them. That is the real significance of the constitutional issue before the country today. Not only has the challenge been made, but we are already "On Our Way."

That a Democratic Administration should repudiate the cardinal principle of States' rights upon which the Democratic Party was founded, and which it has unswervingly defended for a century, and advance the idea of practically wiping out the States in order to centralize power in the Federal Government as an instrument of social and economic control, amounts to a political revolution in itself. But, moreover, we have already seen that the policies of this Administration were not even hinted at in the platform on which it gained office. The Roosevelt regime, once entrenched in power, like its prototypes, embarked on an entirely previously unrevealed program, which is totally different from any ever before professed by any traditional Democrats. Clearly the New Deal is not "Democratic," as "Democratic" has been defined by the recognized leaders—living and dead—of that party. The party machine has been utilized as a political means to power. Historic party principles have been forsaken: the party platform ignored.

The Prophets of the New Deal have invented their own slogans, designed their own symbols, and have written their own program of "professed objectives." Nothing remains now but to destroy the "two-party" system, in order to attain the perfection of the New Despotisms.

We have received an echo from the New Despotisms in the claim that all these extraordinary measures were essential to save America from a violent revolution which was imminent. Possibly they have saved us from a violent revolution (although we doubt if any such was ever threatening), but if so, it has been done by launching a counter-revolution without violence. It seems to us that we have only been given the choice of what kind of revolution we were to have. Certainly the consummation of the "professed objectives" of the Prophets, as we have learned them, are revolutionary in the constitutional and traditional sense. Moreover, the nullification of some of their key emergency measures, the pillars of the bulwark which they erected against this advertised revolution, did not throw us into political chaos or economic disturbances, or into anything which even remotely resembled revolution; on the contrary the country seemed relieved from the uncertainty of experimentation, and business improved. Apparently, therefore, this argument is more "psychological," than real.

To those who claim that the faith of the Founding Fathers and the political institutions of America have become antiquated by human progress we must reply: Why, then, throw us all the way back into the most primitive totalitarian philosophy which civilization has long since not only found antiquated but has emphatically abandoned? The argument would seem to be that because we have not progressed enough, we should destroy all progress. Certainly, the "professed objectives" of these pseudo-modernists are ancient history. They do not give us new truths, they simply masquerade primitive ideas and pagan ideals in modern dress. That seems to be the best they offer us in exchange for what we have. It is not a new theory of government that this country needs, but rather a spiritual renaissance in governmental action and individual conduct: not a reversion to old rejected and alien doctrines, but a rededication to American traditions and ideals.

And so, we conclude, we are at the crossroads in the

journey toward our national destiny: one road is the old American "horse and buggy" road of democracy with the Constitution as its foundation; the other, the foreign slave trail of arbitrary government built upon the arbitrary will of a man or a group of men. Which of these two roads we should take depends entirely upon where we want to go. At any rate, the sign-posts on the road we have been recently traveling should give us a positive understanding of our present direction.

We answer the challenge in the words of Hamilton and Madison, in the Federalist Papers: "An elective despotism was not the government we fought for": and emulating the illustrious example set for us, we "adapt" an historic uterance by inquiring

Delano, Quo Vadis?